SATAKAKĀVYAS OF BHARTṚHARI

Edited & Translated into English

by

Rabindra Kumar Panda

BKP

BHARATIYA KALA PRAKASHAN
DELHI (INDIA)

First Edition : 2006

ISBN : 81-8090-133-5

Published by : **C.P. Gautam**
for **BHARATIYA KALA PRAKASHAN**
3421-A, IInd Floor, Narang Colony,
Tri Nagar, Delhi-110035.
Phone : (O) 27393083, 32967505
(R) 32492129

Laser Typesetting by : Twinkle Graphics, Delhi.

Printed by : BDH Printer at Salasar Imaging System, Delhi-35

Preface

It gives me great pleasure to write few lines at the end of by successful undertaking. I had felt the need of preparing a suitable edition of the *Śatakas* of Bhartṛhari with easy and lucid English translation. No doubt, there are many books on this subject but most of them are long out of print and they have their limitations. The present book has been prepared keeping in view the needs of the students for whom it is prescribed as a text-book by some of the universities, as well as the general lovers of Bhartṛhari's poetry. I have provided a comprehensive introduction which will help the students in understanding and appreciating the merits of Bhartṛhari. I have also supplied the other pertinent lists like the Alphabetical Index of the verses, proverbial expressions, and the list of the metres used by the poet.

Some of the scholars think that the Vijñānaśataka is also composed by Bhartṛhari. I do not accept this. The obvious reason is that it is a substandard production. However, the Vijñānatataka is included in this book as an appendix for ready reference and persual of the critical lovers of poetry.

I have tried my best to make the work as authentic as possible. Proper care has been taken in editing the verses, especially accepting the authentic readings after a serious and careful study of the books of the previous writers. A special mention must be made of B.D. Kosambi whose pioneering critical edition has been very much useful to me. I am, therefore, very much grateful to this eminent scholars who has spent precious portion of life after a critical study of the Śatakas of Bhartṛhari.

I am thankful to C.P. Gautam, the publisher of this book for his care and interest in publishing this book.

R.K. Panda

Contents

Preface .... (*v*)

Introduction .... (*ix*)

1. Nītiśataka
[Sanskrit Text with English Translation] 1

2. Śṛṅgāraśataka
[Sanskrit Text with English Translation] 29

3. Vairāgyaśataka
[Sanskrit Text with English Translation] 57

4. Extra Verses
[with English Translation] 89

5. Appendix I : Vijñānaśatakam 106

6. Alphabetical Index of Verses 121

7. Proverbial Expressions 128

8. Metres in the Śatakas 130

Introduction

Bhartṛhari is one of the best known Sanskrit poets who had made very valuable contribution to the world of human civilisation. Time cannot abolish his name, fame and works. He has been remembered with profound love and respect and will continue to live in the hearts of Indian intellectuals who have realised the value of knowledge and wisdom. We should be proud of the great poet Bhartṛhari who has given us the essence of his wisdom–nectar and guided us to achieve the highest goals of life.

Several centuries have passed since the time of Bhartṛhari, the author of three *Śatakas*. But in the absence of any authentic information, it is difficult to say anything concrete either of Bhartṛhari's life or of his poetical works. Today he is almost a legendary figure. The personal history of Bhartṛhari is not known like those of several luminaries of India. His *Śataka-kāvyas* do not throw any light on his life.

Many stories are being floated among people, which seem to be baseless and of no historical value. According to one story, he was a king and brother of Vikramāditya. He had renounced the world and had became a *Sannyāsin* towards the end of his life. Harihara in his drama *Bhartṛhari-nirveda* presents him as a disciple of Gorakṣanātha from whom he had learnt the science of Yoga. There are Caves in Chunagarh Fort near Banaras, and in Ujjain which are called the caves of Bhartṛhari falling in line with this tradition.

Inguva Rahava Rao in his Introduction to Bhartṛhari's Triśatī in English verse observes :

"Bhartṛhari, the scholar, poet, king and saint, is said to have lived in the first century B.C., when our sub-continent,

India was ruled by several rulers in parts known as kingdoms. Bhartṛhari was the third son of Gandharvasena (as per the traditional accounts) and the other children were Vararuchi, Bhaṭṭi and Vikramaditya. Bhartṛhari after ruling the kingdom for 12 years, took to Sanyāsa, leaving the kingdom to his brother Vikramaditya. There are greatness, his parentage and life. But it is for the historians to throw more light. The cave in Ujjain, where Bhartṛhari is said to have spend his last days after renouncing the kingship, was found in the course of unearthing historical evidences. But like the famous poet Kālidāsa, Bhartṛhari too, had left no account either of his parentage or of his contemporaries. It is evident that he carved a niche rather an immortal place for himself that time cannot wither, and will last till eternity" (p. xvii).

A.A. Macdonell in his Origin and Development of Sanskrit Literature observes :

"The most eminent of these authors (Sanskrit poets who have composed collections of miniature lyrics) is Bhartṛhari, grammarian, philosopher and poet in one. Only the literary training of India could make such a combination possible, and even there it has hardly a parallel. Bhartṛhari lived in the half of the seventh century. The Chinese traveller, I Tsing, who spent more than twenty years in India at the end of that century, records that, having turned Buddhist monk, the poet again became a layman, and fluctuated altogether seven times between the monastery and the world. Bhartṛhari blamed himself for, but could not overcome his inconstancy".

Monier Williams observes :

"Number of wise sayings have, from time immemorial, been constantly quoted in conversation. But occasional attempts were made to give permanence to the floating wisdom of the day, by stringing together in stanzas, the most celebrated maxims and sayings like beads in a necklace, representing a separate topic and the authorship of a whole series being naturally ascribed to men of known wisdom like Bhartṛhari.

Macdonell also remarks :

The proneness of the Indian mind to reflection not only produced important results in religion, philosophy, and science but also found a more abundant expression in poetry than the literature of any other nation can boast. Scattered throughout the most various departments of Sanskrit literature are innumerable apophthegms in which wise and noble, striking and original thoughts often appear in a highly finished and poetical garb." Owing to the universality of this mode of expression in Sanskrit literature, there are but few works consisting exclusively of poetical aphorisms. That most important are the two collections by the high gifted, Bhartṛhari, entitled respectively **Nītiśataka,** or 'Century of conduct,' and **Vairāgya–śataka** or 'Century of Renunciation'. (P. 258).

The keynote prevailing in all this poetry is the doctrine of the vanity of human life which was developed before the rise of Buddhism in the sixth century B.C. and has dominated Indian thought ever since. There is no true happiness, we are here taught, but in the abandonment of desire and retirement from the world. The poet sees the luxuriant beauties of nature spread before his eyes, and feels their charm; but he turns from them sad and disappointed to seek mental calm and lasting happiness in the solitude of the forest. Hence, the picture of a pious anchorite living in contemplation is often painted with enthusiasm. Free from all desires, he is as happy as a king, when the earth is his couch, his arms his pillow, the sky his tent, the moon his lamp, when renunciation is his spouse, and the cardinal points are the maidens that fan him with winds. No Indian poet Inculcates renunciation more forcibly than Bhartṛhari, the humorous and ironical touches which he occasionally introduces are doubtless due to the character of this remarkable man who wavered between the spiritual and the worldly life throughout his carrier.

It is perhaps natural that poetry with a strong pessimistic colouring should contain many bitter sayings about women and their character. At the same time there are some verses in which female character is represented in a more favourable light. As might be expected, true knowledge receives frequent and high appreciation in a Sanskrit ethical poetry. It is compared with a rich treasure which cannot be divided among relations, which no thief can steal and which is never diminished by being imparted to others. The good qualities of the virtuous are often described and contrasted with the characteristics of evil–doers. This, for instance, is how Bhartṛhari, illustrates the humility of the benevolent.

The style of composition of the *Śatakas* is fluent, harmonious and rich in words full of meaning. It is neither artificial nor laboured but chaste, simple and flowing. We observe an accuracy of description of physical phenomena and of their effects delineated by Bhartṛhari. The propositions and general principles have been so lucidly put forward and so well substantiated by instances from everyday life that they readily catch the heart of the reader. Bhartṛhari's verses possess these characteristics to such a degree that they are quoted freely in conversation and didactic discourses, which in itself is no small proof of the richness and superiority of compositions.

A.B. Keith in his *History of Sanskrit Literature, (p. 178)* rightly remarks :

> Bhartṛhari's poetry exhibits Sanskrit to the best advantage. The epics unquestionably lack life and action, their characters are stereotyped, and their descriptions, admirable in detail, tend to be over elaborate and to lose force by this very fact. In Bhartṛhari each stanza normally can stand by itself and serves to express one idea, be it sentiment of love, of resignation, or of policy, in complete and daintily finished form.

The metres adopted in the composition of the verses are small, vigorous and varied, which serve not only to break the monotony but to lend a charm to the composition. Moreover, the verses abound in figures of speech which are so natural and easy that they neither demand any extra- ordinary labour nor great learning from the reader.

The verses composed may be, with stray exceptions by Bhartṛhari himself, cannot be made to give any clue to his individual life, for his poetry seeks to create effect through style and sentiment too conventional to yield themselves to such use. But still his life-long lessons from experience and observation must have been reflected in their peculiar trend and emphasis in the movements of sentiment through the verses; and it may be possible for a reader of penetrative intellect to trace out from such nice shades the bare outline of a deeper life of hard-tought struggles and late won victory. A nature, straight forward, possessed of noble faith in itself, unambitious of high distinction among men, but deeply susceptible to the beauties and charms of sentiment seems to have been involved once in a tangle of sensual enjoyments too heavy to leave it the sustained strength for wielding the scepter, till from a life of such weakness and consequent dependence, it gradually rose through reactions, deep and incisive, to a wonderfully enriched sense of worldly vanity and an effective strength of renunciation. The verses composed by Bhartṛhari tend to present to view the background of such a nature still holding in control lower susceptibilities, once indulged, by the dawning possibilities of a life of Yoga. Though it is difficult to ascertain how for this life of Yoga had advanced behind the role of the poet representing different stages of wisdom it is fairly presumptive that the poet's voice gradually merged in the silence of the highest spiritual realizations.

The epic poem *Rāvaṇavadha* also called after our author as *Bhaṭṭikāvya* is also wrongly ascribed to Bhartṛhari. Bhaṭṭi is the prakritisation of the Sanskrit word *bhartṛ*. The commentators of this poem call him Bhaṭṭi and also Bhartṛhari. For example, Nārāyaṇa-vidyāvinōda in his *Bhaṭṭicandrikā*, Kandarpaśarman in his *Vaijayantī* and Bharatamallika in his *Mugdhabodhinī* call him Bhartṛhari, while Harihara calls him Bhaṭṭi and Jayamaṅgala in his *Jayamaṅgalā* both Bhaṭṭi and Bhartṛhari. The identification of the two Bhartṛharis has arisen because of the similarity in the subject. The *Bhaṭ ṭikāvya* illustrates in its four chapters–*Prakīrṇa, Prasanna, Alaṁkāra* and *Tirianta* the grammatical formations according to the rules of Pāṇini, figures of speech and other poetic devices. There are many stories about this author also. This Bhartṛhari alias Bhaṭṭi is the son of Śrīsvāmin or Śrīdharasvāmin. In the last verse of his *Rāvaṇavadha* he mentions his patron as king Śrīdharasena of Valabhi. The historians are inclined to place the *Bhaṭṭī-kāvya* in the sixth century A.D.

Here it may be noted that the *Subhāṣitatriśatī* and the *Bhaṭṭi-kāvya* are attributed to Bhartṛhari, the grammarian by some individual writers and by tradition. Somadeva (10th cent. A.D.) in his *Yaśastilakacampū* mentions one Bhartṛhari as a *mahākavi,* Merutuṅga (14th cent. A.D.), a Jain writer, mentions in his *Prabodhacintāmaṇi* that the poet Bhartṛhari had written *Vairāgya-śataka* and other poems. Rāmabhadradīkṣita (18th cent.) in his *Patañjalicaritam* (8. 10-11) records a tradition that Bhartṛhari had written the *Śatakas* and the *Vākyapadīya.* Somānanda and Utpalācārya show a verse found in the *Subhāṣitatriśatī* as from the *Śabdadhātusamīkṣā.*

दिक्कालाद्यनवच्छिन्नानन्तचिन्मात्रमूर्तये।
स्वानुभूत्येकमानाय नमः शान्ताय तेजसे॥ *Nīti :* I

But we do not find any reference to *Triśatī* in the extant grammatical works of Bhartṛhari. The critical studies in the *Triśatī* have shown that there were several interpolations with 852 verses against 300 as suggested by the title. Further, I-tsing in his account did not mention about this work while enumerating Bhartṛhari's grammatical works. Therefore the scholars are of the opinion that the author of the *Triśatī* is another Bhartṛhari of a later date.

It is not possible to fix up the chronological order of the *śatakas*. But the subject matter of each of them helps us in guessing that the *Śṛṅgāraśataka* was written first, then the *Nītiśataka* followed by the *Vairāgya-śataka*. The sentiments and ideas pictured in the *Śṛṇgāraśataka* suit the adolescence of youth, those in the *Nītiśataka* are appropriate to middle age, while those in the *Vairāgyaśataka* appear more suited to ripe old age. The first gives expression to feelings and sentiments which arise in the mind when there is buoyancy of spirit, freshness of vigour and vivacity of youth, the second manifests thoughts arising from a deeper insight into the world and its trammels and the third is the outcome of a mind tired and disgusted with the turmoils of mundane material matters seeking repose in renunciation, contentment and quietitude and religion.

The *Nītiśataka* is an endeavour to show the difficulty of the task of bringing fools to their senses, and the various methods resorted to by the greed to acquire wealth, is rich in high sentiments about conduct in this world, such as the nobleness in adhering to promise, the value of learning, self respect, valour, moral courage, and large mindedness. In addition to this, it inculcates principles which will be met with in almost every religion, the importance of industry, the traits of a true friend and a contrast of the conduct of a virtuous and noble hearted man with that of a selfish and little-minded individual. These and other various subjects are so pointedly treated in an epigrammatic form and are of such general applicability that the stanzas will continue to hold a high rank in the literature selected for the inculcation of principles and rules for the conduct of youth in this world.

The *Śṛṅgāraśataka* deals with erotic sentiment by way of describing the beauty of women, their nature, deportment and their effect on the mind of man. The poem also includes a description of the different seasons. The poet has described very nicely the arts by which women captivate the hearts of men. He graphically pictures the effects of all this on the strongest of minds and how they fall victims to the shafts of love. He does not forget to despise harlots and to censure the weakness of man, exhaulting him who stands proof against the wiles and amorous attractions of women.

The *Vairāgyaśataka* abounds in aphorisms holding out the greedy to ridicule and the arrogance of the rich to contempt. It has pointed out in vigorous language the high pressure of physical wants under which the strongest of minds are apt to break but exhorts the reader to a devotion to the supreme truth which is the only controller of all the universe. It exalts in directing man to a renunciation of all worldly matters and seek final beatitude in the great Almighty through his various manifestations. The poem is full of devotion, knowledge and contentment which is its peculiar characteristic. The vividity and accuracy of the scenic descriptions given by him cannot be realised by those who are the slaves of the world and who are panting after its fleeting and ephemeral gains. They can be appreciated by those who have turned aside their minds from all such matters and have devoted themselves to the contemplation of that being providence who is the heaven of all the rich as well as the poor, the happy as well as the distressed.

Budhendra, a commentator of the *Śatakas* of Bhartṛhari, has classified *Nītiśataka* into ten sections called *Paddhatis*. These ten *paddhatis* are *mūrkhapaddhati* (on fools and folly), *vidvatpaddhati* (on wisdom), *māna-śauryapaddhati* (on pride and heroism), *arthapaddhati* (on wealth), *durjanapaddhati* (on the wicked), *sujanapaddhati* (on the good people) *paro-pakārapaddhati* (on virtue), *dhairya paddhati* (on firmness), *daivapaddhati* (on fate), *karma paddhati* (on actions).

The hundred verses of the *Vairāgyaśataka* are divided into ten groups under the following ten headings : तृष्णादूषणम्-condemnation of desire; विषयपरित्यागविडम्बना-futile efforts to give up sense-objects; याच्ञादैन्यदूषणम्-condemnation of the poverty of a suplicant attitude; भोगास्थैर्यवर्णनम्-delineation of the evanescence of enjoyments; कालमहिमानुवर्णनम्-description of the working of Time; यतिनृपतिसंवादवर्णनम्-a comparison as to how a monk stands to a king; मन:संबोधननियमनम्-control of mind by stimulating wisdom in it, नित्यानित्यवस्तुविचार- discrimination of the immutable reality from the mutable; शिवार्चनम्-worship of Śiva; अवधूतचर्या–the way of life for an *Avadhūta* (a self-realized ascetic characterized by the highest spiritual freedom).

1. दिक्कालाद्यन-	स्वभावोक्तिः	अत्र चारुत्वेन यथावद्वस्तुवर्णनात्स्वभावोक्तिरलंकारः स्वभावोक्तिरसौ चारु यथावद्वस्तुवर्णनमिति लक्षणात्।
2. अज्ञः सुखमाराध्यः	अतिशयोक्तिः	रञ्जनसंबन्धेऽप्यसंबन्धाभिधानादतिशयोक्तिभेदः।
3. लभेत सिकतासु	अतिशयोक्तिः	अत्र मण्युद्धरणाद्यसंबन्धेऽपितत्संबन्धाभिधानादतिशयोक्तिः।
4. व्यालं बाल-	निदर्शना	वृत्तिनिदर्शनाभेदः। न चायं दृष्टान्तः। वाक्यभेदेन प्रतिबिम्बकरणाक्षेपे तस्योत्थानात्। अत्र तु वाक्यार्थे वाक्यार्थसमारोपाद्वाक्यैकवाक्यतायां तदभाव इत्यलंकारसर्वस्वकारः।
5. कृमिकुलचितं	अप्रस्तुतप्रशंसा	अत्राप्रस्तुतवृत्तान्तकथनात्प्रस्तुतमूर्खजनप्रतीतेरप्रस्तुतप्रशंसालंकारः।
6. शिरः शार्वं	पर्यायः	अत्रानेकस्मिन्नाधारे क्रमेणैकस्या आधेयभूताया गङ्गायाः स्थितिकथनात्पर्यायाख्योऽलंकारः।
7. हर्तुर्याति	व्यतिरेकः	अत्रोपमानात्प्रसिद्धधनादुपमेयस्य विद्याधनस्याधिक्यकथनाद् व्यतिरेकालंकारः।
8. अम्भोजिनी -	अप्रस्तुतप्रशंसा	अत्राप्रकृतविधातृवृत्तान्तकथनात्प्रस्तुतराजविद्वज्जनप्रतीतेरप्रस्तुतप्रशंसालंकारः।
9. विद्या नाम	निरवयव-रूपकम्	मालारूपकम्। अत्र विद्याया रूपधनाद्याकारेण बहुधा निरूपणान्निरवयवमालारूपकालंकारः।
10. जाड्यं धियो	समुच्चयः	अत्र क्रियाणां बहूनां समुच्चितत्वात्समुच्चयालंकारः।
11. जयन्ति ते	काव्यलिङ्गम्	अत्र रससिद्धपदार्थान्य विशेषणगत्या भावाभावपदार्थं प्रति हेतुत्वात्काव्यलिङ्गभेदः।
12. वहति भुवन -	मालादीपकम्	अत्र पूर्वपूर्वस्योत्तरगुणोत्कर्षावहत्वान्मालादीपकाख्योऽलंकारः।
13. यस्यास्ति	रूपकातिशयोक्तिः	अत्र वित्तस्यैतावद्गुणसंपादकत्वासंबन्धेऽपि तत्संबन्धाभिधानादसंबन्धे संबन्ध रूपातिशयोक्तिः।

14. मणिः शाणो-	दीपकम्	अत्र प्रस्तुतानां नराणां च सामस्त्यार्थ-रूपतुल्यधर्मेणौमम्यस्य गम्यमानत्वाद्दीपकालंकारः।
15. राजन्दुधुक्षसि	संकरः	अत्रस्थोपमया पूर्ववाक्यनिर्व्यूढोत्तर-वाक्यस्थोपमेत्यनयोरङ्गाङ्गिभावेन संकरः।
16. दुर्जनः परिहर्तव्यः	दृष्टान्तः	अत्र बिम्बप्रतिबिम्बन्यायेन धर्मधर्मिणोर्वाक्यद्वये पृथङ्गिर्देशादृष्टान्तालंकारः।
17. मौनान्मूकः	अतिशयोक्तिः	अत्र सेवाधर्मस्य योगिगम्यत्वेऽप्यगम्यत्वोक्तेः संबन्धे असंबन्धरूपातिशयोक्तिः।
18. उद्भासिताखिलः	काव्यलिङ्गम्	अत्रोद्भासितेत्यादि पदार्थस्य विशेषणगत्या सुखस्थित्यभावपदार्थहेतुकत्वात्पदार्थ-हेतुकं काव्यलिङ्गमलंकारः।
19. आरम्भगुर्वी	यथासंख्यम्	अत्र यथासंख्यासंकीर्णोपमालंकारः।
20. मृगमीनसज्जना -	यथासंख्यम्	तृणेन विहितवृत्तीनां मृगाणां लुब्धका निष्कारणवैरिण इत्यादि यथाक्रममन्वयात्क्रमापरनामा यथासंख्यालंकारः।
21. पद्माकरं	यथासंख्यम्	सामान्येन विशेषसमर्थनरूपोऽर्थान्तरन्यासः।
22. क्षीरेणात्मगत-	उत्प्रेक्षा	अत्र स्वभावसिद्धस्य क्षीरनीरव्यवहारस्य परस्परसंतापदर्शनहेतुकत्वेनोत्प्रेक्षणात्क्रियानिमित्तक्रियास्वरूपोत्प्रेक्षा। सा चोक्तार्थान्तरन्यासनिर्व्युढेत्यनयोर्विजातीयसंकरः।
23. इतः स्वपिति	अधिकम्	अत्र लक्षयोजनपरिच्छिन्नस्य समुद्रस्यापरिच्छिन्नकेशवाद्यवतारत्वकथनादधिकप्रभेदोऽलंकारः।
24. जातः कूर्मः	संकरः	रूपकोपमयोः संकरः।
25. नेता यस्य	परिकरः	अत्र साभिप्रायविशेषणत्वात्परिकरालंकारः।
26. या साधूंश्च	विशेषः	अत्र खलादीनां साधुत्वादिकरणादशक्यवस्तुकरणरूपो विशेषालंकारः।
27. आसारेण न	विरोधाभासः	'बत खेदानुकम्पामन्त्रणसन्तोषविस्मये' इत्यभिधानादत्र दुर्दिनमपि सुदिनतां

		यातीति स्फुरते। विरो स्योक्तसमाधानाद्विरोधाभासोऽलंकार:।
28. प्रोद्यत्प्रोढ -	संसृष्टि:	अनुप्रासोपमयो: शब्दार्थालंकारयो: संसृष्टि:।
29. आवास:	संसृष्टि:	अत्र पूवोत्तरवाक्यस्थयोरनुप्रासयमकयो: शब्दालंकारयो: संसृष्टि:।
30. स्मृता भवति	काव्यलिङ्गम्	अत्र 'स्मृता भवति तापाय' इति पदार्थानां विशेषणगत्या तुरीयपादस्थपदार्थं प्रति हेतुत्वात्काव्यलिङ्गभेद:।
31. लीलावतीनां	दृष्टान्त:	अत्र वाक्यद्वयेऽपि बिम्बप्रतिबिम्बभावेन साम्यनिर्देशाद्दृष्टान्तालंकार:।
32. उन्मीलन्त्रि-	रूपकम्	अत्र समस्तवस्तुवर्तिसावयवरूपकालंकार:।
33. व्यादीर्घेण	व्यतिरेक:	अत्र प्रसिद्धाह्यपेक्षया चक्षूरूपाहेराधिक्यकथनाद्व्यतिरेकालंकार:।
34. वेश्यासौ	परिणाम:	अत्र वेश्यायामारोप्यमाणस्य ज्वालात्वस्य प्रकृतहवनोपयोगित्वात्परिणामालंकार:। स च रूपेन्धनेति रूपकेण संकीर्यते रूपकत्वारोपणस्यौपरञ्जकमात्रम्।
35. कश्चुम्बति	संसृष्टि:	अत्र रूपकोपमानुप्रासानां संसृष्टि:।
36. मधु तिष्ठति	संसृष्टि:	अत्रोत्प्रेक्षातिशयोक्तिकाव्यलिङ्गध्वनिभेदानां संसृष्टि:।
37. सहकार	अनुप्रास:	–
38. क्वचित्सभ्रू	उत्प्रेक्षा	तथा नयनवलनक्रियया विकीर्णत्वक्रियोत्प्रेक्षणाद्गुणक्रियानिमित्तक्रियास्वरूपोत्प्रेक्षा।
39. एताश्चलद्व-	संसृष्टि:	अत्र राजहंसीपराजयस्य सादृश्यपर्यवसानादेका उपमा। हरिणीसदृशैरित्यत्र चान्या। अनयो: परस्परनैरपेक्ष्यात्सजातीयसंसृष्टि:।
40. नूनं हि ते	काव्यलिङ्गम्	अत्रोत्तरवाक्यार्थस्य पूर्ववाक्यार्थसमर्थकत्वाद्वाक्यार्थहेतुकं काव्यलिङ्गमलंकार:।

41. नूनमाज्ञाकर-	उत्प्रेक्षा	कामिनीकटाक्षमात्रेणैव जनस्य मन्मथा-वेशसंभवादियमुत्प्रेक्षा। सा च नूनमिति व्यञ्जकसद्भावाद्वाच्या।
42. केशाः संयमिनः	विरोधाभासः संकरः	सा चोक्तरीत्या आभासितत्वाद्विरोधा-भासोऽलंकार। स च श्लेषप्रतिभोत्थापित इति तयोरङ्गाङ्गिभावेन संकरः।
43. सति प्रदीपे	विशेषोक्तिः	अत्रान्धकारनिराकरणसमर्थत्वेन प्रसिद्धे प्रदीपादिकारणसमुदाये सत्यपि तन्निरासरूपकार्यानुत्थानाद्विशेषोक्ति-लंकारः।
44. उद्वृत्त स्तनभारः	संसृष्टिः	अत्र पूर्वार्धे उद्वृत्तत्वादिपदार्थानां श्लेष-भङ्ग्या स्वाभाव्येन च विशेषणगत्या पीडाकरणं पदार्थं प्रति हेतुत्वकथना-त्पदार्थहेतुकमेकं काव्यलिङ्गम्। उत्तरार्धे तु तटस्थपदार्थस्य श्लेषभङ्गैयव केन संतापयतीत्याक्षेपपदार्थं प्रति हेतुत्व-कथनादपरं च। तच्चोक्तोत्प्रेक्षया सापेक्षितत्वात्संकीर्णम्। तत्पूर्ववाक्य-काव्यलिङ्गेन नैरपेक्ष्यात्संसृज्यत इत्यनयोः सजातीयसंसृष्टिः।
45. मुखेन चन्द्र	श्लेषः	
46. संसारेऽस्मिन्न-	काव्यलिङ्गम्	अत्रोत्तरवाक्यार्थस्य पूर्व-वाक्यार्थ-समर्थकहेतुत्वात्काव्यलिङ्गभेदः।

Some of the Alaṁkāras are explained in the following pages :

Viṣama - Alaṅkāra

भोगा न भुक्ता वयमेव भुक्ता -
स्तपो न तप्तं वयमेव तप्ताः।
कालो न यातो वयमेव याता -
स्तृष्णा न जीर्णा वयमेव जीर्णाः॥ *(Vairāgyaśatuka, 7)*

(The worldly pleasures have not been enjoyed by us, but we ourselves have devoured; no religious austerities have been gone through, but we ourselves have become scorched; time is not gone (being ever present and infinite), but it is we who are gone (because of approaching death). Desire is not reduced in force, though we ourselves are reduced to senility).

Here there is an ironical pun on the participles भुक्ता and तप्ता the former being used both in the sense of "enjoyed" and "eaten up", and the latter both in the sense of "austerities performed" and "heated". Similarly the participle जीर्णा means both "reduced in force" and "stricken down with age."

Parikara

परेषां चेतांसि प्रतिदिवसमाराध्य बहुधा
प्रसादं किं नेतुं विशसि हृदय क्लेशकलिलम्।
प्रसन्ने त्वय्यन्तः स्वयमुदितचिन्तामणिगणे
विविक्तः संकल्पः किमभिलषितं पुष्यति न ते॥

(*Vairāgyaśataka*)

Parikara is a speech with significant epithets. The above is an example :

Oh mind! instead of flattering others you be yourself satisfied. Trying to please others is not independent; it is fraught with difficulties, while it is within your own control to be content and thereby to secure the fountain of all happiness.

The verse contains *parikara-alaṅkāra,* for it contains the significant epithets namely, क्लेशकलिलम्, चिन्तामणि and विविक्तः।

The first epithet means a chaotic mass of troubles. स्वयमुदितचिन्तामणिगुण means 'having the virtue of a philosopher's stone developed of itself in you – *i.e.,* one of the eight yogic powers, प्राप्तिः. विविक्त we prefer to render as 'free from the is implied when we have to depend on others for gratifying our desires.

Mālānidarśanā

व्यालं बालमृणालतन्तुभिरसौ रोद्धुं समुज्जृम्भते
भेत्तुं वज्रमणिं शिरीषकुसुमप्रान्तेन संनह्यते।
माधुर्यं मधुबिन्दुना रचयितुं क्षाराम्बुधेरीहते
मूर्खान्यः पथि नेतुमिच्छति बलात्सूक्तैः सुधास्यन्दिभिः॥

(*Nītiśataka,* verse 6)

This verse is an example of मालानिदर्शना (garland of illustrations). According to Mammaṭa, when a connection of impossible things implies a comparison it is called *nidarśanā.* When the *upamānas* are numerous it becomes *mālānidarśanā.* (निदर्शना, अभवन्वस्तुसम्बन्ध उपमापरिकल्पकः॥ अनेकोपमानयोगान्मालारूपाप्येषा शेया। KP. In the present instance, a connection is established between the *upameya viz.,* desire to lead the wicked into the path of the virtuous and the *upamānas viz.,* curbing a maddened elephant by means of tender lotus filaments, cutting the diamond with a petal of a śirīṣa flower, sweetenning the salt waters of the ocean by means of a drop of honey.

Vikalpa

तपस्यन्तः सन्तः किमधिनिवसामः सुरनदीं
गुणोदारान्दारानुत परिचरामः सविनयम्।

पिबामः शास्त्रौघानुत विविधकाव्यामृतरसा-
न्न विद्मः किं कुर्मः कतिपयनिमेषायुषि जने॥

(*Vairāgyaśataka, 76)*

(Shall we live by the celestial river practising austerities, or shall we amiably serve our wives graced by virtues; shall we drink of the currents of scriptural literature, or of the nectar of diverse poetical literature? Man having the longevity of a few twinklings of the eye, we do not know which (of these) to undertake!

The verse contains the *alaṅkāra* called *vikalpa*.

Saṅkara

मोहं मार्जय तामुपार्जय रतिं चन्द्रार्धचूडामणौ
चेतः स्वर्गतरङ्गिणीतटभुवामासङ्गमङ्गीकुरु।
को वा वीचिषु बुद्बुदेषु च तडिल्लेखासु च श्रीषु च
ज्वालाग्रेषु च पन्नगेषु च सरिद्वर्गेषु च प्रत्ययः॥

(*Vairāgyaśataka, 64*)

(Clear off delusion and earn devotion to Him whose crown is begemmed with the crescent. Oh heart, accept attachment to some spot on the banks of the celestial river Ganges. What reliability is there on waves or bubbles, flashes of lightning or smiles of fortune, in tongues of flame, serpents or hosts of friends?) The verse is having *Saṅkara-alaṅkāra* of *dīpaka* and *Tulyayogītā.*

Praharṣaṇa

भग्नाशस्य करण्डपिण्डिततनोर्म्लानेन्द्रियस्य क्षुधा
कृत्वाखुर्विवरं स्वयं निपतितो नक्तं मुखे भोगिनः।
तृप्तस्तत्पिशितेन सत्वरमसौ तेनैव यातः पथा
स्वस्थास्तिष्ठत दैवमेव हि परं वृद्धौ क्षये कारणम्॥

(Nitiśataka, 82)

(A serpent who was confined in a basket where in his

body was squeezed and whence he had lost all hope of escape, was half dead with hunger. Once on a night, a rat made a hole in the basket (through which he got in) and fell into the jaws of the serpent. The latter revived by the rat's flesh speedily made *hi* exit by the same path (by which the rat had entered). Oh people! behold, fate alone is the cause of the decline and prosperity of men.)

This verse contains *Praharṣaṇa-alaṅkāra* because here the eagernes of the serpent to escape and get food is described as fulfilled without any effort.

उत्कण्ठितार्थसंसिद्धिर्विना यत्नं प्रहर्षणम्
Mammaṭa includes this *alaṅkāra* in *Samādhi.*

Viṣādanam

खल्वाटो दिवसेश्वरस्य किरणैः संतापिते मस्तके
गच्छन्देशमनातपं द्रुतगतिस्तालस्य मूलं गतः।
तत्राप्यस्य महाफलेन पतता भग्नं सशब्दं शिरः
प्रायो गच्छति यत्र दैवहतकस्तत्रैव यान्त्यापदः॥
(Nitiśataka, 84)

(A bald-headed man was scroched on his head by the rays of the sun and being anxious to find a shady place went, under the influence of fate, to the foot of a palm tree while there, a large fruit of the tree fell on his head making a loud noise and broke it. Generally calmities follow the unfortunate man wherever he may happen to go.)

इष्यमाणविरुद्धार्थसंप्राप्तिस्तु विषादनम्।

Svabhāvokti

लाङ्गूलचालनमधश्चरणावपातं
भूमौ निपत्य वदनोदरदर्शनं च।
श्वापिण्डदस्य कुरुते गजपुंगवस्तु
धीरं विलोकयति चाटुशतैश्च भुङ्क्ते॥ *(Nitiśataka, 84)*

Svabhāvokti is the description of the action, color and figure peculiar to a child and other things. In this verse we get an *alaṅkāra* called *svabhāvokti* which is defined as स्वभावोक्तिस्तु डिम्भादेः स्वक्रियारूपवर्णनम्। KP. Here is a description of the characteristic action and posture of the dog and the elephant. It is also an *anyokti* or *anyāpadeśa*.

Dṛṣṭānta (Exemplification)

न कश्चिच्चण्डकोपानामात्मीयो नाम भूभुजाम्।
होतारमपि जुह्वानं स्पृष्टो दहति पावकः॥ *(Nitiśataka, 46)*

Dṛṣṭānta is the reflective representation of the common attribute, the object of comparison and the standard of comparison. The above verse contains *dṛṣṭānta-alaṅkāra.*

Pratīpam

लोभश्चेदगुणेन किं पिशुनता यद्यस्ति किं पातकैः
सत्यं चेत्तपसा च किं शुचि मनो यद्यस्ति तीर्थेन किम्।
सौजन्यं यदि किं निजैः स्वमहिमा यद्यस्ति किं मण्डनैः
सद्विद्या यदि किं धनैरपयशो यद्यस्ति किं मृत्युना॥

(Nītiśatakam, 55)

(What other vice is there beyond avarice, what sin can be worse than slandering, what worth of penances when there is veracity, what is the need of a sacred place to the pure mind, what need of relatives if there is civility, what better ornament than one's own fame, what value of wealth when there is learning and where remains the fear of death after disgrace).

The *alaṅkāra* that is present in this verse is प्रतीप which defined as आक्षेप उपमानस्य प्रतीपम् (K.P.)

In this verse the *Upamānas aguṇa*, namely *pātaka* etc. are condemned since the *upameyastobha.* etc. are considered quite capable of serving the purpose of the *upamānas.*

Kāvyaliṅga

जातिर्यातु रसातलं गुणगणस्तस्याप्यधो गच्छतां
शीलं शैलतटात्पतत्वभिजनः संदह्यतां वह्निना।
शौर्ये वैरिणि वज्रमाशु निपतत्वर्थोऽस्तु नः केवलं
येनैकेन विना गुणास्तृणलवप्रायाः समस्ता अमी।।

(Nitiśataka, 31)

The above verse has *kāvyaliṅga-alaṅkāra* for the phrase येनैकेन etc. constitutes the reason for desiring wealth only regardless of *jāti* etc.

When a reason is implied in a sentence or a word, it is termed *kāvyaliṅga.* It should be noted that it is a productive (*kāraka*) *hetu* which is the province of *kāvyaliṅga*, while an indicative or informative (*jñāpaka*) *hetu* forms *anumāna*. The reason in this figure is poetical, and not a logical one.

Some more examples are :

गुणवदगुणवद्वा कुर्वता कार्यमादौ
परिणतिरवधार्या यत्नतः पण्डितेन।
अतिरभसकृतानां कर्मणामाविपत्ते-
र्भवति हृदयदाही शल्यतुल्यो विपाकः।। *(Nitiśataka, 95)*

यस्यास्ति वित्तं स नरः कुलीनः
स पण्डितः स श्रुतवान्गुणज्ञः।
स एव वक्ता स च दर्शनीयः
सर्वे गुणाः काञ्चनमाश्रयन्ते।। *(Nitiśataka, 32)*

In this stanza the phrase सर्वे गुणाः काञ्चनमाश्रयन्ते explains the reason why a person having wealth is considered कुलीन, पण्डित, &c.

शशिदिवाकरयोर्ग्रहपीडनं
गजभुंजगमयोरपि बन्धनम्।
मतिमतां च विलोक्य दरिद्रतां
विधिरहो बलवानिति मे मतिः।। *(Extra Verses, 26)*

In this stanza the last line विधिरहो बलवानिति मे मतिः (the thought strikes me-how powerful is fate!) gives the reason why the sun and the moon are exposed to the assaults of Rāhu, why there are bonds of the elephant and the serpent, why are wise men in poverty.

Vibhāvanā

When an effect is said to arise without a cause, it is *vibhāvanā*. In *vibhāvanā*, the ordinary well-known cause of an effect being absent, it comes into existence owing to the operation of some extraordinary cause which is not so well-known or so easily conceived. The following verse is an example :

करे श्लाघ्यस्त्यागः शिरसि गुरुपादप्रणयिता
मुखे सत्या वाणी विजयि भुजयोर्वीर्यमतुलम्।
हृदि स्वच्छा वृत्तिः श्रुतमधिगतं च श्रवणयो-
र्विनाप्यैश्वर्येण प्रकृतिमहतां मण्डनमिदम्॥ *(Nitiśataka, 46)*

Vibhāvanā-alaṅkāra is found in the present verse because *maṇḍana* (adornment) is narrated without *aiśvarya* (pomp).

Yathāsaṁkhya

मृगमीनसज्जनानां तृणजलसंतोषविहितवृत्तीनाम्।
लुब्धकधीवरपिशुना निष्कारणमेव वैरिणो जगति॥

(Nitiśataka, 50)

(The deer, the fish, and the good people are (respectively) satisfied with grass, water, and anything that may be got by chance; still in this world the huntsman, the fisherman and the wicked are their wanton enemies.)

The verse contains *yathāsaṁkhya-alaṅkāra* which is defined by Mammaṭa as यथासंख्यं क्रमेणैव क्रमिकाणां समन्वयः। (K.P.). In this verse *lubdhaka, dhīvara,* and *piśuna* are mentioned as the enemies of *mṛga, mīna* and *sajjana* respectively.

Prativastūpamā

अधिगतपरमार्थान्पण्डितान्मावमंस्था-
स्तृणमिव लघु लक्ष्मीर्नैव तान्संरुणद्धि।
अभिनवमदरेखाश्यामगण्डस्थलानां
न भवति बिसतन्तुर्वारणं वारणानाम्।। (*Nitiśataka, 13)*

The trait of not being brought under restraint by insignificant objects which is common to the *upamāna* and *upameya* is expressed by separate phrases in the stanza. Hence the *alaṁkāra* is *prativastūpamā.*

The above verse is a beautiful example of *Prativastūpamā* which is defined as Bhartṛhari was tremendous impact on the later rhetoricians who had cited his verses in their poetic works. We are trying to give here some of the examples.

Siṁhabhūpāla, the author of the *Rasārṇavasudhākara* cites the following verse :

दीना दीनमुखैः स्वकीयशिशुकेराकृष्टजीर्णाम्बरा
क्रोशद्भिः क्षुधितैर्निरन्नपिठरा नैक्ष्येत चेद् गेहिनी।
याच्ञादैन्यभयेन गद्गदगलत्रुय्यद्विलीनाक्षरं
को देहीति वदेत् स्वदग्धजठरस्यार्थे मनस्वी पुमान्।।
(*Vairāgyaśataka, 21)*

It is given as an example of *dainya, a vyabhicāribhāva* caused by *daurgatya.*

हृत्तापदुर्गतत्वाद्यैरनौद्धत्यं हि दीनता।।
तत्रानुभावा मालिन्यगात्रस्तम्भादयो मताः।। (P. 152)

प्राप्ताः श्रियः सकलकमदुघास्ततः किं
न्यस्तं पदं शिरसि विद्विषतां ततः किम्।
संपादिताः प्रणयिनो विभवैस्ततः किं
कल्पस्थितास्तनुभृतां तनवस्ततः किम्।।
(*Vairāgyaśataka*, 67)

Siṁhabhūpāla cites the verse twice in his *Rasārṇavasudhākara* p. 149 :

(Though embodied beings obtain that prosperity from which all desires are milked, what then? What if their feet be placed on the heads of their enemies? Or what if their wealth brings friends, or if their bodies endure till the end of the creative cycle?

First, as an example, of *nirveda,* a *vyabhicāribhāva* which is caused by *tattvajñāna* (तत्त्वज्ञानाच्च दौर्गत्यादापदो विप्रयोगतः, p. 149)

Secondly, as an example of *nirveda.*

अत्र निर्वेदस्यानन्याङ्गत्वात् स्वतन्त्रत्वम्
स्वातन्त्र्यात् पारतन्त्र्याच्च ते द्विधा व्यभिचारिणः। (P. 149)
परपोषकतां प्राप्ताः परतन्त्रा इतीरिताः
तदभावे स्वतन्त्राः स्युभावा इति च ते स्मृताः॥ (P. 204-5)

It is interesting to note that in both the places readings in the second and the third lines are different.

न्यस्तं पदं शिरसि विद्विषतां ततः किम्
संमानिताः प्रणयिनो विभवैस्ततः किं। (P. 149)
संमानिताश्च विभवैः सुहृदस्ततः किम्
न्यस्तं पदं शिरसि विद्विषतां ततः किम्॥ (P. 205)

Siṁhaphūpāla cites the following verse :

अशीमहि वयं भिक्षामाशावासो वसीमहि।
शयीमहि महीपृष्ठे कुर्वीमहि किमीश्वरैः॥

from the *Vairāgyaśataka* (55) as an example of *dhṛti,* a *vyabhicāribhāva* which is caused by cognition (*jñāna*). *Dhṛti* is defined as :

ज्ञानविज्ञानगुर्वादिभक्तिनानार्थसिद्धिभिः।
लज्जादिभिश्च चित्तस्य नैस्पृह्यं धृतिरुच्यते॥ (P. 189)

Viśvanātha in his *Sāhityadarpaṇa* cites the following verse :

शशी दिवसधूसरो गलितयौवना कामिनी
सरो विगतवारिजं मुखमनक्षरं स्वाकृतेः।
प्रभुर्धनपरायणः सततदुर्गतः सज्जनो
नृपाङ्गनगतः खलो मनसि सप्त शल्यानि मे॥

(*Nitiśataka, 45*)

as an example of सदसद्योग-समुच्चयालंकार from the *Nītiśataka.* Each one of the above is capable of causing great pain to the mind; this being so, many others are mentioned as producing the same effect. Therefore the figure is *sammucaya*. The word सदसद्योग may be explaind in two ways : सन्तश्च असन्तश्च a combination of good things with other things that are bad: or सन्तश्च ते असन्तश्च (कर्मधारय) तेषां योगः, a combination of things that are both good and bad (*i.e.,* that are good in one way and bad in another). The first explanation of सदसद्योग is resorted to by some who say that in शशी etc. the moon and others are good and the wicked man is bad and thus there is a combination of good and bad things. There are three objcctions against this view. Firstly, there is no charm in the combination of the moon etc. with the खल. Secondly, the concluding words of the stanza are against the above construction. All the seven objects are declared to be शल्यऽ; so the moon etc. cannot be शोभन. Thirdly, if we take this interpretation the word सदसद्योग, we shall commit the fault of सहृयरभिन्नता। A combination of good things with bad things, instead of being an ornament, is a fault.

Some of the poeticians have also found faults in the verses of Bhartṛhari. For example,

Raghunāṭha Manohara in his *Kavikaustubha* has shown *Yatibhraṣṭa* fault in the following verse of the *Nītiśataka,* verse 5 :

लभेत सिकतासु तैलमपि यत्नतः पीडय-
न्पिबेच्च मृगतृष्णिकासु सलिलं पिपासार्दितः।
कदाचिदपि पर्यटञ्शशविषाणमासादये-
न्नतु प्रतिनिविष्टमूर्खजनचित्तमाराधयेत्॥

This verse is composed in Pṛthvī metre and its *yati* should be on 8th and 17th syllable of the lines. Here *yati* on the word तै ल of the first line and मूर्ख on the fourth line. It leads to the metrical fault called *yatibhraṣṭa.*

अत्र प्रथमचतुर्थचरणयोर्यतिभङ्गे, उक्तं च छन्दोरत्नावल्याम्-
सखे यदि च षष्ठकं तदनु चाष्टकं द्वादशं
द्वितीयमपि यत्र वा गुरु च षोडशाद्यान्त्यगौ।
चतुर्दशमथ क्रमात् सकलभाग्यवारांनिधे
श्रुतिद्वयस्तीसृपैर्विरतिरङ्ग पृथ्वी मता॥

अत्र पृथ्वीछन्दसि श्रुतिद्वयसरीसृपैरष्टनवभिरक्षरैर्यतिरिति व्याख्या-यां सत्यां, सिकतासु तैलमित्यत्र प्रतिनिविष्टमूर्खजनचित्तमित्यत्र यतिचिच्छेदा-द्यतिभ्रष्टदोषः। (P. 92)

(Tripathi, Chandrashekhar, *Kavikaustubha*, Vidyanidhi Prakashan, Delhi, 2001.)

Erotic (Śṛṅgāra)

Both love in union **(Sambhoga)** and love in separation **(Vipralambha)** are found in the **Śṛṅgāra–Śataka** of Bhartṛhari.

Rasadhvani

अदर्शने दर्शनमात्रकामा
दृष्ट्वा परिष्वङ्गरसैकलोला।
आलिङ्गितायां पुनरायताक्ष्या-
माशास्महे विग्रहयोरभेदम्॥ (*Śṛṅgāraśataka, verse 22*)

सति प्रदीपे

सति प्रदीपे सत्यग्नौ सत्सु तारारवीन्दुषु।
विना मे मृगशावाक्ष्या तमोभूतमिदं जगत्॥

The verse contains *viśeṣokti–alaṁkāra*. It also has *vastudhvani.*

तथा प्रदीपादिसद्भावेऽपि तमोभूतत्वमिति विरोधच्च व्यज्यते। तेन चास्य महामोहान्धत्वं वस्तु गम्यत इत्यलंकारेण वस्तुध्वनिः। (65)

अपसर सखे

अपसर सखे दूरादस्मात्कटाक्षविषानला-
त्प्रकृतिविषमाद्योषित्सर्पाद्विलासफणाभृतः।
इतरफणिना दष्टः शक्यश्चिकित्सितुमौषधै-
श्चतुरवनिताभोगिग्रस्तं त्यजन्ति हि मन्त्रिणः॥

अत्रापि समस्तवस्तुवर्तिसावयवरूपकालंकारः। तेन चोपमानात्प्रसिद्ध-सर्पादुपमेयस्य योषित्सर्पस्याधिक्यप्रतीतेर्व्यतिरेको व्यज्यत इत्यलंकारेणालंकार ध्वनिः। (85)

मुग्धे धानुष्कता केयमपूर्वा त्वयि दृश्यते।
यया विध्यसि चेतांसि गुणैरेव न सायकैः॥

(*Śṛṅgāraśataka, verse 13*)

अत्र पूर्ववाक्यार्थस्योत्तरवाक्यार्थसमर्थितत्वाद्वाक्यार्थहेतुकं काव्यलिङ्गम्। तच्च गुणयोः श्लेषभित्तिकाभेदाध्यवसायमूलातिशयोक्तिनिर्व्यूढ मित्यनयोरङ्गा-गिभावेन संकरः। तेन च प्रसिद्धाद्धानुष्कादुपमानादुपमेयभूतमुग्धाया आधिक्य-प्रतीतेर्व्यतिरेको व्यज्यत इत्यलंकारेणालंकारध्वनिः। (64)

Kaiśikivṛtti

कुङ्कुमपङ्कलङ्कितदेहा
गौरपयोधरकम्पितहारा।
नूपुरहंसरणत्पदपद्मा
कं न वशीकुरुते भुवि रामा॥ (*Śṛṅgāraśataka, 9*)

अत्र श्लाघ्यविशेषणयोगादुदात्ततानामा गुणः। तथात्यन्तसुकुमारार्थ-संदर्भितत्वात्कैशिकी वृत्तिः–'अत्यन्तसुकुमारार्थसंदर्भा कैशिकी मता।'

क्वचित्सभ्रू

क्वचित्सभ्रूभङ्गैः क्वचिदपि च लज्जापरिगतैः
क्वचिद्धूरित्रस्तैः क्वचिदपि च लीलाविलसितैः।
कुमारीणामेतैर्मदनसुसगैर्नेत्रवलितैः
स्फुरन्नीलाब्जानां प्रकरपरिकीर्णा इव दिशः।

(*Śṛṅgāraśataka, 4*)

संसारे स्वप्नसारे परिणतितरले द्वे गती पण्डितानां
तत्त्वज्ञानामृताम्भःप्लवललितधियां यातु कालः कथंचित्।
नो चेन्मुग्धाङ्गनानां स्तननाभोगसंभोगिनीनां
स्थूलोपस्थस्थलीषु स्थगितकरतलस्पर्शलीलोद्यमानाम्॥

(*Śṛṅgāraśataka, 37*)

वा पण्डितानां कालो यापयितव्यः। न त्वन्यथेति भावः। स्थूलोपस्थेत्यनेन आसां चित्रिणीजातित्वं सूचितम्। तदुक्तं रतिरहस्ये–'मदनसदनमस्या वर्तुलोच्छूनमन्तर्मृदु मदनजलाढ्यं रोमभिर्नातिसान्द्रैः। प्रकृतिचपलदृष्टिर्बाह्यसंभोगसक्ता रसयति मधुराल्पं चित्रिणी चित्ररक्ता॥' इति। एतज्जात्यनुकूलसुरतनियतयामोऽपि तत्रैवोक्तः–'व्रजति रतिसुखार्थी चित्रिणीमग्रयामे भजति दिनरजन्योर्हस्तिनीं च द्वितीये। गमयति च तृतीये शङ्खिनीमार्द्रभावां रमयति रमणीयां पद्मिनीं तुर्ययामे॥' इति। मतान्तरे तु द्वितीययाम इत्युक्तम्–'घनकुचनखभेदैर्मुष्टिघातैश्च मध्ये रतिनियतकरेश्च प्रीतियुक्तैर्वचोभिः। अनृततरकथाभिस्तत्र यामे द्वितीये सुगुणसहितमन्तश्चित्रिणीं संलभेत॥'

स्मितं किंचिन्मुग्धं

स्मितं किंचिन्मुग्धं सरलतरलो दृष्टिविभवः
परिस्पन्दो वाचामभिनवविलासोक्तिसरसः।
गतानामारम्भः किसलयितलीलापरिकरः
स्पृशन्त्यास्तारुण्यं किमिव न हि रम्यं मृगदृशः॥

(*Śṛṅgāraśataka, 6*)

इयं मुग्धा नायिका–'उदयद्योवना मुग्धा लज्जाविजितमन्मथा' इति लक्षणात्। (P. 60)

एताश्चलद्व

एताश्चलद्वलयसंहतिमेखलोत्थ-
झंकारनूपुररवाहृतराजहंस्यः।
कुर्वन्ति कस्य न मनो विवशं तरुण्यो
वित्रस्तमुग्धहरिणीसदृशैः कटाक्षैः॥ (*Śṛṅgāraśataka, 8*)

एताश्च मध्यमा नायिकाः—लज्जामन्मथमध्यस्था मध्यमोदितयौवना' इति लक्षणात्।

Udātta

स्मितं किंचिन्मुग्धं सरलतरलो दृष्टिविभवः
परिस्पन्दो वाचामभिनवविलासोक्तिसरसः।
गतानामारम्भः किसलयितलीलापरिकरः
स्पृशन्त्यास्तारुण्यं किमिव न हि रम्यं मृगदृशः॥

(*Śṛṅgāraśataka, 6*)

अत्र श्लाघ्यविशेषणयोगादुदात्तता नाम गुणः—'श्लाघ्यैर्विशेषणैर्योगो यस्याश्च स्यादुदात्तता' इति लक्षणात्॥ (P. 60)

Bhartṛhari is a past master in mythological allusions. While illustrating some object or person, he moulds his examples so as they become an adjective of a mythological personality.

His allusions have become a part and parcel of his verses and do not appear to be superfluous. Most of his mythological allusions are derived from the *Rāmāyaṇa*, the *Mahābhārata* and the *Purāṇas*.

Brahmā

ब्रह्मापि नरं न रञ्जयति। NŚ. 3.d.

स्वायत्तमेकान्तहितं विधात्रा। NŚ. 7.a.

हंसस्य हन्ति नितरां कुपितो विधाता। NŚ. 14.b.

यद्धात्रा निजभालपट्ट.................... NŚ. 40.a.

ब्रह्मा येन कुलालवन्नियमितो.......... NŚ. 92.a.

Rudraṭa has described two types of **anumāna alaṁkāra.** In the second type first *sādhya* is described and then **sādhana**. The example is given in the Hindi–commentary of Acharya Viśveśvara Siddhanta Siromani.

मधु तिष्ठति वाचि – P. 523.

प्राप्ता श्रियः – P. 333.

Mammaṭa has quoted the following :

शशी दिवसधूसर–as an example of samuccayaalaṁkāra (असतां योगः)

अत्र शशिनि धूसरे शल्ये शल्यान्तराणीति शोभनाशोभनयोगः। P. 516.

Thus the verses of Bhartṛhari are sweet and charming. They possess extra-ordinary merits. Their melodious flow, rhythemic style and musical arrangement of words easily attract the hearts of the readers.

१

नीतिशतकम्

दिक्कालाद्यनवच्छिन्नानन्तचिन्मात्रमूर्तये।
स्वानुभूत्येकमानाय नमः शान्ताय तेजसे॥१॥

We offer our obeisance to the peaceful light, whose form is only of pure intelligence, unlimited and unconditioned by space, time, etc., and the principal means of which is self-experience.

बोद्धारो मत्सरग्रस्ताः प्रभवः स्मयदूषिताः।
अबोधोपहताश्चान्ये जीर्णमङ्गे सुभाषितम्॥२॥

Learned men are under the influence of envious feelings, men of position are spoilt through pride and the rest are smitten by ignorance, the precepts do remain in.

अज्ञः सुखमाराध्यः सुखतरमाराध्यते विशेषज्ञः।
ज्ञानलवदुर्विदग्धं ब्रह्मापि नरं न रञ्जयति॥३॥

An ignorant man can be easily propitiated, a wise man can still more easily propitiated but even Brahmā cannot please that man who is puffed up with a little knowledge.

प्रसह्य मणिमुद्धरेन्मकरवक्त्रदंष्ट्रान्तरा-
त्समुद्रमपि सन्तरेत्प्रचलदूर्मिमालाकुलम्।
भुजङ्गमपि कोपितं शिरसि पुष्पवद्धारये-
न्न तु प्रतिनिविष्टमूर्खजनचित्तमाराधयेत्॥४॥

One may forcibly recover a jewel from the tip of the tongue of a crocodile; he may even swim across the sea whose waters are agitated by a series of waves in motion; he may as well wear an excited serpent on his head like a flower but he cannot win over the perverse mind of a fool.

लभेत सिकतासु तैलमपि यत्नतः पीडय-
न्पिबेच्च मृगतृष्णिकासु सलिलं पिपासार्दितः।
कदाचिदपि पर्यटञ्शशविषाणमासादये-
न्न तु प्रतिनिविष्टमूर्खजनचित्तमाराधयेत्॥५॥

A man may get even oil from sand by strennuous pressure; when oppressed by thirst he may drink water from the mirage; while he may per chance even come across the horn of a hare in wandering; but he can never win the obstinate mind of a fool.

व्यालं बालमृणालतन्तुभिरसौ रोद्धुं समुज्जृम्भते
भेत्तुं वज्रमणिं शिरीषकुसुमप्रान्तेन संनह्यते।
माधुर्यं मधुबिन्दुना रचयितुं क्षाराम्बुधेरीहते
मूर्खान्यः पथि नेतुमिच्छति बलात्सूक्तैः सुधास्यन्दिभिः॥६॥

He who wishes to lead the wicked into the path of the virtuous by sweet persuasive language is like one who endeavours to carb a maddened elephant by means of tender lotus filament. He is like one who tries to cut the diamond with the edge of the Śīrīṣa flower or like one who hopes to sweeten the salt waters of the ocean by means of a drop of honey.

स्वायत्तमेकान्तहितं विधात्रा
विनिर्मितं छादनमज्ञतायाः।
विशेषतः सर्वविदां समाजे
विभूषणं मौनमपण्डितानाम्॥७॥

The creator has created a certain and effective means to disguise ignorance which can be readily commanded , *viz.* silence which, especially in an assembly of learned men, becomes a befitting ornament to ignorant folks.

यदा किंचिज्ज्ञोऽहं द्विप इव मदान्धः समभवं
तदा सर्वज्ञोऽस्मीत्यभवदवलिप्तं मम मनः।
यदा किंचित्किंचिद्बुधजनसकाशादवगतं
तदा मूर्खोऽस्मीति ज्वर इव मदो मे व्यपगतः॥८॥

When I was knowing a little, I was blinded by pride as an elephant and my mind was puffed up with the idea that I know everything. When, however, I gradually gained knowledge through the contact of the wise men, I came to know that I was a fool; and the pride, which had possessed me like a fever, vanished.

कृमिकुलचितं लालाक्लिन्नं विगन्धि जुगुप्सितं
निरुपमरसप्रीत्या खादन्नरास्थि निरामिषम्।
सुरपतिमपि श्वा पार्श्वस्थं विलोक्य न शङ्कते
न हि गणयति क्षुद्रो जन्तुः परिग्रहफल्गुताम्॥९॥

A dog, even if sees the lord of the Heaven (Indra) standing by him, does not hesitate to devour with unparalleled relish and delight a human bone destitute of flesh, full of clusters of vermin, emitting a loathsome stench, disgusting, and covered with saliva. Verily a mean man does not give thought to the worthlessness of what he has come by.

शिरः शार्वं स्वर्गात्पशुपतिशिरस्तः क्षितिधरं
महीध्रादुत्तुङ्गादवनिमवनेश्चापि जलधिम्।
अधो गङ्गा सेयं पदमुपगता स्तोकमथ वा
विवेकभ्रष्टानां भवति विनिपातः शतमुखः॥१०॥

The Gaṅgā falls from heaven on the head of Śiva, from the head of Śiva to the mountain, from that lofty mountain to the earth and from thence to the ocean. Thus falling lower and lower this river does come to an insignificant position : that wonder, in a variety of ways comes about the fall of those who are devoid of all sense.

शास्त्रोपस्कृतशब्दसुन्दरगिरः शिष्यप्रदेयागमा
विख्याताः कवयो वसन्ति विषये यस्य प्रभोर्निर्धनाः।
तज्जाड्यं वसुधाधिपस्य सुधियस्त्वर्थं विनापीश्वराः
कुत्स्याः स्युः कुपरीक्षकैर्न मणयो यैरर्धतः पातिताः॥११॥

When learned men of cellebrity, whose speech adorned with words polished by the śāstras and whose learning is fit to be imparted to pupils, have to live in poverty in the kingdom of a prince, then that betrays the folly of the ruler, for the learned are respected even without wealth. If jewels are priced lower than their due worth the blame is attached to the incompetent examiners but not to the jewels.

हर्तुर्याति न गोचरं किमपि शं पुष्णाति यत्सर्वदा-
प्यर्थिभ्यः प्रतिपाद्यमानमनिशं प्राप्नोति वृद्धिं पराम्।
कल्पान्तेष्वपि न प्रयाति निधनं विद्याख्यमन्तर्धनं
येषां तान्प्रति मानमुज्झत नृपाः कस्तैः सह स्पर्धते॥१२॥

Oh kings! cast off your pride before those who possess the sacret treasure of wisdom, a treasure which does not come within the scope of the thief, which always imparts indescribable happiness, which largely increases though it is constantly given to those who desire it and which is not destroyed even at the time of universal destruction. Who can compere with such persons?

अधिगतपरमार्थान्पण्डितान्मावमंस्था-
स्तृणमिव लघु लक्ष्मीर्नैव तान्संरुणद्धि।
अभिनवमदरेखाश्यामगण्डस्थलानां
न भवति बिसतन्तुर्वारणं वारणानाम्॥१३॥

Do not despise wise men who have acquired knowledge. The worthless lucre is as insignificant as a blade of grass. It does not tie them down. The filament of a lotus-stalk does not restrain to elephants whose temples are blackened with the streaks of fresh rut.

अम्भोजिनीवनविलासनिवासमेव
हंसस्य हन्ति नितरां कुपितो विधाता।
न त्वस्य दुग्धजलभेदविधौ प्रसिद्धां
वैदग्ध्यकीर्तिमपहर्तुमसौ समर्थः॥१४॥

Highly irritated Bramhā can destroy swan's enjoyment of residing in beds of lotuses in a pond, but he cannot deprive him of his fame about the natural skill of separating milk from water.

केयूराणि न भूषयन्ति पुरुषं हारा न चन्द्रोज्ज्वला
न स्नानं न विलेपनं न कुसुमं नालंकृता मूर्धजाः।
वाण्येका समलंकरोति पुरुषं या संस्कृता धार्यते
क्षीयन्ते खलु भूषणानि सततं वाग्भूषणं भूषणम्॥१५॥

Neither do bracelets, nor necklaces brilliant like the moon, nor bath nor annointing (of perfumes), nor flowers, nor decorated hair, become ornaments to a man; but it is his polished speech which adorns him. Adornments are, in fact destructible, but eloquence is an everlasting ornament.

विद्या नाम नरस्य रूपमधिकं प्रच्छन्नगुप्तं धनं
विद्या भोगकरी यशःसुखकरी विद्या गुरूणां गुरुः।
विद्या बन्धुजनो विदेशगमने विद्या परं दैवतं
विद्या राजसु पूज्यते न तु धनं विद्याविहीनः पशुः॥१६॥

Learning, indeed, imparts high splendour to a man; it is a valuable treasure which is concealed and well-guarded; it is a means of securing glory and ease, it is the greatest of the greats, it is a friend in travelling through foreign lands, and it is the supreme divinity. Learning, not wealth, is highly honoured by kings. A man without learning is but a brute.

क्षान्तिश्चेत्कवचेन किं किमरिभिः क्रोधोऽस्ति चेद्देहिनां
ज्ञातिश्चेदनलेन किं यदि सुहृद्दिव्यौषधैः किं फलम्।
किं सर्पैर्यदि दुर्जनाः किमु धनैर्विद्यानवद्या यदि
व्रीडा चेत्किमु भूषणैः सुकविता यद्यस्ति राज्येन किम्॥१७॥

If a man has patience what is the need of an armour, if he

has anger what other enemy need he fear. If he has relatives what is the need of fire, if he has a true friend what use has he of medicines of potent virtue; if there are bad people with him why should he fear serpents; if he has flawless learning what worth are riches to him, if he has sense of shame what other ornament does he require; if he has good poems what pleasure can he have from a kingdom.

दाक्षिण्यं स्वजने दया परिजने शाठ्यं सदा दुर्जने
प्रीतिः साधुजने नयो नृपजने विद्वज्जनेष्वार्जवम्।
शौर्यं शत्रुजने क्षमा गुरुजने नारीजने धूर्तता
ये चैवं पुरुषाः कलासु कुशलास्तेष्वेव लोकस्थितिः॥१८॥

Indulgence towards one's own people, kindness to strangers, caution with respect to the wicked, love for the good people, politic behaviour with kings, straight forwardness in dealing with the learned, bravery with enemies, forbearance towards elders, shrewdness with regard to those who are versed in those arts, are the persons on whom the preservation of social order rests.

जाड्यं धियो हरति सिञ्चति वाचि सत्यं
मानोन्नतिं दिशति पापमपाकरोति।
चेतः प्रसादयति दिक्षु तनोति कीर्तिं
सत्संगतिः कथय किं न करोति पुंसाम्॥१९॥

Say, what the company of the good people does not do? It removes the dulness of the intellect, instils varacity in the speech, directs to the loftiness of self-respect, removes sinful tendencies, purifies the mind and also spreads the fame in all directions.

जयन्ति ते सुकृतिनो रससिद्धाः कवीश्वराः।
नास्ति येषां यशःकाये जरामरणजं भयम्॥२०॥

Victorious are the poets-in-chief conversant with all sentiments, whose bodies in the form of fame enjoy immunity from old age and death.

क्षुत्क्षामोऽपि जराकृशोऽपि शिथिलप्रायोऽपि कष्टां दशा–
मापन्नोऽपि विपन्नदीधितिरपि प्राणेषु नश्यत्स्वपि।
मत्तेभेन्द्रविभिन्नकुम्भपिशितग्रासैकबद्धस्पृहः
किं जीर्णं तृणमत्ति मानमहतामग्रेसरः केसरी॥२१॥

The lion, the foremost among the prouds, has unparalleled eagerness for swallowing a mouthful–out of the temples broken by himself of a great intoxicated elephant does although emaciated by hunger, weakened by old age, almost exhausted and come to a miserable plight, with all his vigour gone, and even on the verge of death ever feed upon withered grass?

स्वल्पं स्नायुवसावसेकमलिनं निर्मांसमप्यस्थि गोः
श्वा लब्ध्वा परितोषमेति न च तत्तस्य क्षुधाशान्तये।
सिंहो जंबुकमङ्कमागतमपि त्यक्त्वा निहन्ति द्विपं
सर्वः कृच्छ्रगतोऽपि वाञ्छति जनः सत्त्वानुरूपं फलम्॥२२॥

A dog rejoices over a little bone destitute of flesh and filthy with small remains of tendons and fat on it, though it does not appease his hunger. But a lion rejects a jackal even though it comes under his paw and kills only an elephant. Each one sets his desire on an object according to his inborn nature although he may be in distress.

लाङ्गूलचालनमधश्चरणावपातं
भूमौ निपत्य वदनोदरदर्शनं च।
श्वा पिण्डदस्य कुरुते गजपुंगवस्तु
धीरं विलोकयति चाटुशतैश्च भुङ्क्ते॥२३॥

A dog wags his tail, falls at the feet of his master and exhibts his mouth and belly falling on the ground; but a lordly elephant looks grave and eats after hundreds of flattering words.

परिवर्तिनि संसारे मृतः को वा न जायते।
स जातो येन जातेन याति वंशः समुन्नतिम्॥२४॥

In this ever changing world who is not born and who does not die. He is really born by whose birth the family is raised to great prosperity.

कुसुमस्तबकस्येव द्वयी वृत्तिर्मनस्विनः।
मूर्ध्नि वा सर्वलोकस्य शीर्यते वन एव वा॥२५॥

The position of the high-minded people is two-fold as in the case of a bunch of flowers, either to be on head of the people, or to wither away in a forest.

सन्त्यन्येऽपि बृहस्पतिप्रभृतयः संभाविताः पञ्चषा-
स्तान्प्रत्येष विशेषविक्रमरुची राहुर्न वैरायते।
द्वावेव ग्रसते दिनेश्वरनिशाप्राणेश्वरौ भास्वरौ
भ्रातः पर्वणि पश्य दानवपतिः शीर्षावशेषीकृतः॥२६॥

There are some five or six planets with Bṛhaspati as their head, who are held in esteem. Rāhu desirous of figuring in special valour does not show enmity towards any of them. The lord of the demons (Rāhu) though has nothing left of his form except his head, devours at conjunction and opposition only the splendid ruler of day and the lord of night. Mark this, oh brother!

वहति भुवनश्रेणीं शेषः फणाफलकस्थितां
कमठपतिना मध्येपृष्ठं सदा स च धार्यते।
तमपि कुरुते क्रोडाधीनं पयोधिरनादरा-
दहह महतां निःसीमानश्चरित्रविभूतयः॥२७॥

The Śeṣa bears the several regions of the world on the flat of his hood, he is constantly borne by the king of the tortoise on his back who, in his turn, is again held without difficulty by the ocean on his breast. Ah! boundless is the brilliancy of the performances of the greats.

वरं पक्षच्छेदः समदमघवन्मुक्तकुलिश-
प्रहारैरुद्गच्छद्बहुलदहनाद्गारगुरुभिः।
तुषाराद्रेः सूनोरहह पितरि क्लेशविवशे
न चासौ संपातः पयसि पयसां पत्युरुचितः॥२८॥

Better for the son of the Himālaya to have allowed his wings to be cut off by the proud Indra by strokes of his thunder-bolt which became unbearable on account of their emitting huge masses of flame; but alas! his throwing himself in the waters of the ocean and seeking refuge there was improper when his father was overwhelmed by calamity.

यदचेतनोऽपि पादैः स्पृष्टः प्रज्वलति सवितुरिनकान्तः।
तत्तेजस्वी पुरुषः परकृतनिकृतिं कथं सहते॥२९॥

Even the insentient sun-jewel emits burning heat when touched by the feet (the rays) of the sun. How can a man of mettle then tolerate an insult made by others?

सिंहः शिशुरपि निपतति मदमलिनकपोलभित्तिषु गजेषु।
प्रकृतिरियं सत्त्ववतां न खलु वयस्तेजसो हेतुः॥३०॥

A lion, though infant, attacks elephants whose rampart like temples are soiled with rut. This is the nature of valiant. Age, indeed, is not the cause of valour.

जातिर्यातु रसातलं गुणगुणस्तस्याप्यधो गच्छतु
शीलं शैलतटात्पतत्वभिजनः संदह्यतां वह्निना।
शौर्ये वैरिणि वज्रमाशु निपतत्वर्थोऽस्तु नः केवलं
येनैकेन विना गुणास्तृणलवप्रायाः समस्ता अमी॥३१॥

Let caste go to the nether world, let the aggregate of virtues sink lower still, let goodness of character fall from a precipice, let nobility be burnt down with fire; let the thunderbolt strike at once, bravery which is not friend (to us); wealth alone is ours, without which all these virtues are like a piece of straw.

यस्यास्ति वित्तं स नरः कुलीनः
स पण्डितः स श्रुतवान्गुणज्ञः।
स एव वक्ता स च दर्शनीयः
सर्वे गुणाः काञ्चनमाश्रयन्ति॥३२॥

That man who possesses wealth is well-born, he is learned, he is an appreciator of merits, he alone is eloquent and handsome. All virtues attach themselves to gold.

दौर्मन्त्र्यान्नृपतिर्विनश्यति यतिः सङ्गात्सुतो लालना-
द्विप्रोऽनध्ययनात्कुलं कुतनयाच्छीलं खलोपासनात्।
ह्रीर्मद्यादनवेक्षणादपि कृषिः स्नेहः प्रवासाश्रया-
न्मैत्री चाप्रणयात्समृद्धिरनयात्त्यागात्प्रमादाद्धनम्॥३३॥

A king on account of evil counsel, an anchorite by attachment to worldly pleasures, a son by indulgence, a brahmin by not studying the Vedas, a family by a misbehaved son, a character by association with the wicked; modesty by wine, husbandry by want of attentionl affection by resorting to travel, friendship by want of courtesy, prosperity by bad management, and wealth by misdirected charity are ruined.

दानं भोगो नाशस्तिस्त्रो
गतयो भवन्ति वित्तस्य।
यो न ददाति न भुंक्ते
तस्य तृतीया गतिर्भवति॥३४॥

Charity, enjoyment and destruction are the three courses of wealth. He who neither gives nor enjoys looses his wealth.

मणिः शाणोल्लीढः समरविजयी हेतिदलितो
मदक्षीणो नागः शरदि सरिदाश्यानपुलिनाः।
कलाशेषश्चन्द्रः सुरतमृदिता बालवनिता
तनिम्ना शोभन्ते गलितविभवाश्चार्थिषु नराः॥३५॥

A jewel cut on a polishing-stone, a conqueror wounded by weapons, an elephant weakened by passion, rivers with their sandy banks laid bare in autumn, the moon slendered into a crescent, a young damsel languid through enjoyment appear beautiful by their slenderness. Same is the case with persons whose wealth has been diminished by being given to the needy.

परिक्षीणः कश्चित्स्पृहयति यवानां प्रसृतये
स पश्चात्संपूर्णः कलयति धरित्रीं तृणसमाम्।
अतश्चानेकान्ता गुरुलघुतयार्थेषु धनिना-
मवस्था वस्तूनि प्रथयति च संकोचयति च॥३६॥

A poor, who longs for a handful of rice regards the whole

earth as straw. Hence we must say that (the position of the wealthy magnifies or lessens their value) for want of fixity as regards the smallness or largeness of the objects of desire.

राजन्दुधुक्षसि यदि क्षितिधेनुमेनां
तेनाद्य वत्समिव लोकमिमं पुषाण।
तस्मिंश्च सम्यगनिशं परिपोष्यमाणे
नानाफलं फलति कल्पलतेव भूमिः॥३७॥

O king, if you wish to milk this cow-earth then, you first nourish the nation which is like a calf. When the nation is being constantly enriched, the earth like the desire-granting creeper, yields a variety of fruits.

सत्याऽनृता च परुषा प्रियवादिनी च
हिंस्त्रा दयालुरपि चार्थपरा वदान्या।
नित्यव्यया प्रचुरनित्यधनागमा च
वाराङ्गनेव नृपनीतिरनेकरूपा॥३८॥

The policy of kings is like a courtesan who has manifold appearances false and true; harsh and pleasant, cruel and merciful, at one time covetuous and at another liberal; either always squandering money or continuously heaping it together.

आज्ञा कीर्तिः पालनं ब्राह्मणानां
दानं भोगो मित्रसंरक्षणं च।
येषामेते षड्गुणा न प्रवृत्ताः
कोऽर्थस्तेषां पार्थिवोपाश्रयेण॥३९॥

What is the use of those people becoming the king's servants who do not possess these six qualities *viz.* the power, fame, the of Brāhmaṇas, charity, the enjoyment of pleasures and the protection of friends.

यद्धात्रा निजभालपट्टलिखितं स्तोकं महद्वा धनं
तत्प्राप्नोति मरुस्थलेऽपि नितरां मेरौ च नातोऽधिकम्।
तद्धीरो भव वित्तवत्सु कृपणां वृत्तिं वृथा मा कृथाः
कूपे पश्य पयोनिधावपि घटो गृह्णाति तुल्यं जलम्॥४०॥

The amount of wealth that is written on the forehead by

fate whether little or much, is gained even in a desert but not a little more even on the mount of Meru. Be patient and do not unnecessarily adopt a humiliating conduct. Look at a jar which takes up the same quantity of water from well and from the ocean.

अकरुणत्वमकारणविग्रहः
परधने परयोषिति च स्पृहा।
सुजनबन्धुजनेष्वसहिष्णुता
प्रकृतिसिद्धमिदं हि दुरात्मनाम्॥४१॥

Cruelty, causeless quarrels, desire for another's wife and wealth, envy of the good people and relatives are the natural chracteristics of the wicked people.

दुर्जनः परिहर्तव्यो विद्ययालंकृतोऽपि सन्।
मणिना भूषितः सर्पः किमसौ न भयंकरः॥४२॥

A wicked man should be avoided though adorned with learning. Is not a serpent decked with a jewel dangerous?

जाड्यं ह्रीमति गण्यते व्रतरुचौ दम्भः शुचौ कैतवं
शूरे निर्घृणता मुनौ विमतिता दैन्यं प्रियालापिनि।
तेजस्विन्यवलिप्तता मुखरता वक्तर्यशक्तिः स्थिरे
तत्को नाम गुणो भवेत्सुगुणिनां यो दुर्जनैर्नाङ्कितः॥४३॥

Evil-minded persons ascribe dulness to the shy, hypocrisy to one who has a liking for rigid vows, deceit in the case of the pure-minded, cruelty to the brave, ignorance to one given to meditation, servility with reference to the courteous, pride to the sprited, prattling to the eloquent, feebleness to the steady. What trait, then, in persons, possessed of good qualities is not branded by the wicked?

लोभश्चेदगुणेन किं पिशुनता यद्यस्ति किं पातकैः
सत्यं चेत्तपसा च किं शुचिमनो यद्यस्ति तीर्थेन किम्।
सौजन्यं यदि किं निजैः स्वमहिमा यद्यस्ति किं मण्डनैः
सद्विद्या यदि किं धनैरपयशो यद्यस्ति किं मृत्युना॥४४॥

If one has avarice why should he require other bad qualities;

if one has wickedness, why should he want sins; if one has truthfulness, why should he practise religious austerities; if one has purity of heart what is the use of pilgrimage? If one has goodness of heart, why should he want relatives? If one has reputation, what is the use of ornaments. If one possesses learning, what is the use of wealth? If one has a bad name why should he need death?

शशी दिवसधूसरो गलितयौवना कामिनी
सरो विगतवारिजं मुखमनक्षरं स्वाकृतेः।
प्रभुर्धनपरायणः सततदुर्गतिः सज्जनो
नृपाङ्गणगतः खलो मनसि सप्त शल्यानि मे॥४५॥

These are seven thorns to my mind. The moon obscured by day-light, a woman who has lost her youth, a pond destitute of lotuses, a handsome person without education, a prince entirely devoted to money, a good man always put in difficulties, and an evil man frequenting a king's court.

न कश्चिच्चण्डकोपानामात्मीयो नाम भूभुजाम्।
होतारमपि जुह्वानं स्पृष्टो दहति पावकः॥४६॥

Kings full of wrath have verily none whom they call their own. The sacred fire burns even the priest who usually offers oblations if he happens to touch it.

मौनान्मूकः प्रवचनपटुर्वाचको जल्पको वा
धृष्टः पार्श्वे भवति च वसन्दूरतोऽप्यप्रगल्भः।
क्षान्त्या भीरुर्यदि न सहते प्रायशो नाभिजातः
सेवाधर्मः परमगहनो योगिनामप्यगम्यः॥४७॥

The of service is most difficult to understand; it is beyond the ken of even sages. A servant is called dumb if he is silent, if he is ready with his answer, he is said to be talkative and gurrulous if he stands near, he is impudent; if he keeps at a distance, he is timid; if he bears patiently, he is a coward; and if he cannot tolerate (insults) he is generally considered unmannerly.

उद्भासिताखिलखलस्य विशृङ्खलस्य
प्राग्जातविस्मृतनिजाधमकर्मवृत्तेः।
दैवादवाप्तविभवस्य गुणद्विषोऽस्य
नीचस्य गोचरगतैः सुखमास्यते कैः॥४८॥

Who can live happily within the range of a wicked man who hates merit, who has by chance attained greatness, and has forgotten his former mode of obtaining a living by base deeds, and who is free from all restraint, has white-washed all other wicked people.

आरम्भगुर्वी क्षयिणी क्रमेण
लघ्वी पुरा वृद्धिमती च पश्चात्।
दिनस्य पूर्वार्धपरार्धभिन्ना
छायेव मैत्री खलसज्जनानाम्॥४९॥

The friendship between good man and bad man differs as widely as the shadow (of an object) in the first half and the latter half of the day. In the first case it appears great at the commencement and gradually diminishes. In the second, it is small at first and goes on increasing.

मृगमीनसज्जनानां तृणजलसंतोषविहितवृत्तीनाम्।
लुब्धकधीवरपिशुना निष्कारणमेव वैरिणो जगति॥५०॥

The deer, the fish, and the virtuous, living on grass, water and contentment respectively have in this world unprovoked enemies as the hunter, the fisherman and the wicked.

वाञ्छा सज्जनसंगमे परगुणे प्रीतिर्गुरौ नम्रता
विद्यायां व्यसनं स्वयोषिति रतिर्लोकापवादाद्भयम्।
भक्तिः शूलिनि शक्तिरात्मदमने संसर्गमुक्तिः खलै-
रेते येषु वसन्ति निर्मलगुणास्तेभ्यो महद्भ्यो नमः॥५१॥

A bow to those men in whom reside the following sterling qualities : desire for the company of virtuous, satisfaction at the merits of others, humility towards elders, attachment to learning, love for one's own wife, fear of calumny, devotion to the Trident-holder (Śiva), strength to restrain the self and freedom from the company of wicked men.

विपदि धैर्यमथाभ्युदये क्षमा
सदसि वाक्पटुता युधि विक्रमः।
यशसि चाभिरतिर्व्यसनं श्रुतौ
प्रकृतिसिद्धमिदं हि महात्मनाम्॥५२॥

Firmness in adversity, forbearance in prosperity, eloquence in an assembly, bravery in battle, desire for glory, devotion for the Vedas, are the natural characteristics of the high minded people.

करे श्लाघ्यस्त्यागः शिरसि गुरुपादप्रणयिता
मुखे सत्या वाणी विजयि भुजयोर्वीर्यमतुलम्।
हृदि स्वच्छा वृत्तिः श्रुतमधिगतं च श्रवणयो-
र्विनाप्यैश्वर्येण प्रकृतिमहतां मण्डनमिदम्॥५३॥

Liberality is the fitting virtue for the hand, bowing at the feet of elders for the head, true speech for the mouth, incomparable prowess for valiant arms, pure feeling for the heart, the acquisition of the Śāstras for the ears are the adornments of persons who are naturally great even without any other pomp.

प्राणाघातान्निवृत्तिः परधनहरणे संयमः सत्यवाक्यं
काले शक्त्या प्रदानं युवतिजनकथामूकभावः परेषाम्।
तृष्णास्त्रोतो विभङ्गो गुरुषु च विनयः सर्वभूतानुकम्पा
सामान्यं सर्वशास्त्रेष्वनुपहतविधिः श्रेयसामेष पन्थाः॥५४॥

Abstinence from destroying life, restraint in depriving others of their wealth, speaking the truth, timely liberality according to one's power, not even gossiping about the young ladies of others, checking the stream of covetuousness, reverence for elders, compassion towards all creatures is the universal path to happiness violating no rules or ordinances of any śāstra.

संपत्सु महतां चित्तं भवत्युत्पलकोमलम्।
आपत्सु च महाशैलशिलासंघातकर्कशम्॥५५॥

The mind of great men becomes soft like a lotus in prosperity and becomes hard like a solid rock in adversity.

प्रिया न्याय्या वृत्तिर्मलिनमसुभङ्गेऽप्यसुकरं
त्वसन्तो नाभ्यर्थ्याः सुहृदपि न याच्यः कृशधनः।
विपद्युच्चैः स्थैर्यं पदमनुविधेयं च महतां
सतां केनोद्दिष्टं विषममसिधाराव्रतमिदम्॥५६॥

A course of conduct pleasing and upright at once, not stooping to a sinful act even when life is in danger, never to supplicate the wicked nor to beg of a friend who has very little wealth, living nobly in adversity, and following the footsteps of the great by whom this vow, as difficult to perform as walking on the edge of a sword, has been tought to the good?

प्रदानं प्रच्छन्नं गृहमुपगते संभ्रमविधिः
प्रियं कृत्वा मौनं सदसि कथनं चाप्युपकृतेः।
अनुत्सेको लक्ष्म्यां निरभिभवसाराः परकथाः
सतां केनोद्दिष्टं विषममसिधाराव्रतमिदम्॥५७॥

Secret generosity, cheerful hospitality to strangers arrived at one's house, doing good to others and being silent about it, but proclaiming among people the benefits received from others, absence of pride in prosperity, speaking of others in terms free from contempt : Who has taught to the good this excessively difficult conduct as sharp as the edge of a sword?.

संतप्तायसि संस्थितस्य पयसो नामापि न श्रूयते
मुक्ताकारतया तदेव नलिनीपत्रस्थितं दृश्यते।
अन्तःसागरशुक्तिकुक्षिपतितं तन्मौक्तिकं जायते
प्रायेणाधममध्यमोत्तमजुषामेवंविधा वृत्तयः॥५८॥

Not the least trace of water is found when it falls upon heated iron; the same, lying on a lotus leaf, shines assuming the form of pearls. It is also transformed into a pearl when it falls into the cavity of the shells in the sea. Perhaps the lowest, the mediocre and the highest degrees of excellence arise out of association.

यः प्रीणयेत्सुचरितैः पितरं स पुत्रो
यद्भर्तुरेव हितमिच्छति तत्कलत्रम्।
तन्मित्रमापदि सुखे च समक्रियं य-
देतत्त्रयं जगति पुण्यकृतो लभन्ते॥५९॥

He who makes his parents happy by his good character is son, she who wishes the well-being of her husband is wife, he is a friend who is behaves equally at the time of happiness and misery. A person who has done enough *puṇya* obtains all these three things in this world.

नम्रत्वेनोन्नमन्तः परगुणकथनैः स्वान्गुणान्ख्यापयन्तः
स्वार्थान्संपादयन्तो विततपृथुतरारम्भयत्नाः परार्थे।
क्षान्त्यैवाक्षेपरूक्षाक्षरमुखरमुखान्दुर्जनान्दुःखयन्तः
सन्तः साश्चर्यचर्या जगति बहुमताः कस्य नाभ्यर्चनीयाः॥६०॥

Those who are ennobled by humility, who display their own virtues by relating the virtues of others, who achieve their own objects by extended efforts in large deeds undertaken for others, who rebuke, only by their patience, evil-speakers whose mouths are full of harsh and slanderous words, are the persons of admirable conduct commanding the respect of all in this world. Who would not respect them?

भवन्ति नम्रास्तरवः फलोद्गमै-
र्नवाम्बुभिर्दूरविलम्बिनो घनाः।
अनुद्धताः सत्पुरुषाः समृद्धिभिः
स्वभाव एवैष परोपकारिणाम्॥६१॥

Trees become bend with the harvest of fruits; the clouds hang very low with newly formed waters; good men (with the acquisition of) wealth become meek; this is the nature of benevolent persons.

श्रोत्रं श्रुतेनैव न कुण्डलेन
दानेन पाणिर्न तु कङ्कणेन।
विभाति कायः करुणाकुलानां
परोपकारेण न चन्दनेन॥६२॥

The ear is graced by vedic knowledge alone, not by an ear-ring; the hand by charity, not by a bracelet; the body of beneficent people by kindness towards others, not by sandal-paint.

पद्माकरं दिनकरो विकचं करोति
चन्द्रो विकासयति कैरवचक्रवालम्।
नाभ्यर्थितो जलधरोऽपि जलं ददाति
सन्तः स्वयं परहिते विहिताभियोगाः॥६३॥

The sun opens the groups of lotuses, the moon expands a group of kairava lotuses, the cloud gives water even without being asked. The good men are of their own accord perseveringly devoted to the interest of others.

एते सत्पुरुषाः परार्थघटकाः स्वार्थान्परित्यज्य ये
सामान्यास्तु परार्थमुद्यमभृतः स्वार्थाविरोधेन ये।
तेऽमी मानुषराक्षसाः परहितं स्वार्थाय निघ्नन्ति ये
ये निघ्नन्ति निरर्थकं परहितं ते के न जानीमहे॥६४॥

Those men are good who accomplish the good qualities of others disregarding their own; those are ordinary men who devote themselves to do good to others in a manner as not to clash with their own interests; those are monsters in human form who destroy the good of others for their own profit. However, we do not know what to call them who aimlessly cause injury to another's prospects.

पापान्निवारयति योजयते हिताय
गुह्यं निगूहति गुणान्प्रकटीकरोति।
आपद्गतं च न जहाति ददाति काले
सन्मित्रलक्षणमिदं प्रवदन्ति सन्तः॥६५॥

Wise people thus describe the characteristics of a true friend; he dissudes (you) from sin, urges (you) to good action, keeps (your) secrets, publishes (your) merits, does not forsake in distress, and helps you in time of need.

क्षीरेणात्मगतोदकाय हि गुणा दत्ताः पुरा तेऽखिलाः
क्षीरोत्तापमवेक्ष्य तेन पयसा स्वात्मा कृशानौ हुतः।
गन्तुं पावकमुन्मनस्तदभवद्दृष्ट्वा तु मित्रापदं
युक्तं तेन जलेन शाम्यति सतां मैत्री पुनस्त्वीदृशी॥६६॥

Milk, at first, imparted all (its) qualities to its constituent water; on seeing the distress of milk (*i.e.* when it was heated) water sacrificed itself in the fire (*i.e.* became evaporated); seeing the distress of its friend (*i.e.* water); it (*viz.* milk) became very eager to throw itself into the fire (lit. to go to the fire, *i.e.* began to boil over); but it settled down when united with that water. Such is the friendship of the good people.

इतः स्वपिति केशवः कुलमितस्तदीयद्विषा–
मितश्च शरणार्थिनां शिखरिणां गणाः शेरते।
इतोऽपि वडवानलः सह समस्तसंवर्तकै–
रहो विततमूर्जितं भरसहं च सिन्धोर्वपुः॥६७॥

Oh what wonder! How wide, powerful and mighty is the expense of the ocean, (for) on one side of it sleeps Keśava, on the other there is the host of enemies of his followers; in one place lie the numerous mountains seeking shelter, in another there is the submarine fire with all the fires of destruction.

जातः कूर्मः स एकः पृथुभुवनभरायार्पितं येन पृष्ठं
श्लाघ्यं जन्म ध्रुवस्य भ्रमति नियमितं यत्र तेजस्विचक्रम्।
संजातव्यर्थपक्षाः परहितकरणे नोपरिष्टान्न चाधो
ब्रह्माण्डोदुम्बरान्तर्मशकवदपरे जन्तवो जातनष्टाः॥६८॥

That Tortoise alone was born who offered his back for the heavy burden of the world; the birth of Dhruva (alone) is to be praised regulated by whom the planetary system revolves; other creatures in the world are, like the insects in an *udumbara* fruit, which possesses wings to no purpose, as it were born and dead (simultaneously), since they are not in any way useful to others (and since) (both) the present world and the next have become unavailable to them.

तृष्णां छिन्धि भज क्षमां जहि मदं पापे रतिं मा कृथाः
सत्यं ब्रूह्यनुयाहि साधुपदवीं सेवस्व विद्वज्जनम्।
मान्यान्मानय विद्विषोऽप्यनुनय प्रख्यापय प्रश्रयं
कीर्तिं पालय दुःखिते कुरु दयामेतत्सतां लक्षणम्॥६९॥

Restrain desire, cultivate forbearance, leave of pride, have no inclination for evil deeds, speak the truth, follow the path of the *rightous,* seek the company of the learned, honour the respectable, appease even enemies, conceal your own virtues, guard your reputation, be kind to the distressed good. These are the characteristics of the good people.

मनसि वचसि काये पुण्यपीयूषपूर्णा–
स्त्रिभुवनमुपकारश्रेणिभिः प्रीणयन्तः।
परगुणपरमाणून्पर्वतीकृत्य नित्यं
निजहृदि विकसन्तः सन्ति सन्तः कियन्तः॥७०॥

In this world, what a small number is there of good men whose thoughts, words and persons, are as if filled with nectar in the form of meritorious deeds, who please the three worlds with numerous benevolent actions and who are always enlivened in their minds by exalting even the very smallest virtues of another to the size of a mountain.

रत्नैर्महाब्धेस्तुतुषुर्न देवा
न भेजिरे भीमविषेण भीतिम्।
सुधां विना न प्रययुर्विरामं
न निश्चितार्थाद्विरमन्ति धीराः॥७१॥

With the acquisition of valuable jewels the gods were not satisfied and at the dread poison they were not terrified; they did not stop working until they obtain nectar. Resolute persons do not swerve from a policy once determined upon.

प्रारभ्यते न खलु विघ्नभयेन नीचैः
प्रारभ्य विघ्नविहता विरमन्ति मध्याः।
विघ्नैर्मुहुर्मुहुरपि प्रतिहन्यमानाः
प्रारब्धमुत्तमगुणा न परित्यजन्ति॥७२॥

For fear of obstacles, nothing is begun at all by persons who are low-spirited, ordinary people begin and stop when thwarted by difficulties; but the best men, though repeatedly repelled by adverse circumstances, do not give up what they have once undertaken.

लज्जां गुणौघजननीं जननीमिवार्या-
मत्यन्तशुद्धहृदयामनुवर्तमानाः।
तेजस्विनः सुखमसूनपि संत्यजन्ति
सत्यव्रतव्यसनिनो न पुनः प्रतिज्ञाम्॥७३॥

Spirited men who are devoted to the resolution of being truthful, readily give up even their life rather than swerve from their word which to them is like their own mother who instils the sense of shame and various other qualities is perfectly pure-hearted, and wholly devoted to them.

क्वचिद् भूमौ शायी क्वचिदपि च पर्यङ्कशयनः
क्वचिच्छाकाहारः क्वचिदपि च शाल्योदनरुचिः।
क्वचित्कन्थाधारी क्वचिदपि च दिव्याम्बरधरो
मनस्वी कार्यार्थी गणयति न दुःखं न च सुखम्॥७४॥

A man of constant mind resolved upon securing his own object does care neither for happiness nor for misery at one time he may lie on the ground, at another he may sleep on a couch; he may live on vegetables, or on cooked rice of superior variety; sometimes, he may wear a patched quilt of rags and at others a magnificent garment.

निन्दन्तु नीतिनिपुणा यदि वा स्तुवन्तु
लक्ष्मीः समाविशतु गच्छतु वा यथेष्टम्।
अद्यैव वा मरणमस्तु युगान्तरे वा
न्याय्यात्पथः प्रविचलन्ति पदं न धीराः॥७५॥

Let men versed in policy praise or blame, let the goddess

of wealth enter or go away as she likes, let death come even today or in any day. Persons of mental calibre do not swerve from the path of justice.

कान्ताकटाक्षविशिखा न लुनन्ति यस्य
चित्तं न निर्दहति कोपकृशानुतापः।
कर्षन्ति भूरिविषयाश्च न लोभपाशा
लोकत्रयं जयति कृत्स्नमिदं स धीरः॥७६॥

That courageous man conquers all the three worlds, whose mind through the arrow-like side-glances of women do not hurt, the heat of fire like anger does not burn and the numerous sensual objects do not draw with their captivating snares.

कदर्थितस्यापि हि धैर्यवृत्ते-
र्न शक्यते धैर्यगुणं प्रमार्ष्टुम्।
अधोमुखस्यापि कृतस्य वह्ने-
र्नाधः शिखा यान्ति कदाचिदेव॥७७॥

The virtue of courage of a heroic person cannot be obliterated though is worried; the flame of fire does not point to the ground though pointed downwards.

गजभुजंगविहंगमबन्धनं शशिदिवाकरयोर्ग्रहपीडनम्।
मतिमतां च समीक्ष्य दरिद्रतां विधिरहो बलवानिति मे मतिः॥७८॥

'Fate is the most powerfun one' is my assumption and that is observed from the bondage of elephant, snake and birds, suffering of the moon and the sun by the planets and the poverty of the wise men.

वह्निस्तस्य जलायते जलनिधिः कुल्यायते तत्क्षणा-
न्मेरुः स्वल्पशिलायते मृगपतिः सद्यः कुरङ्गयते।
व्यालो माल्यगुणायते विषरसः पीयूषवर्षायते
यस्याङ्गेऽखिललोकवल्लभतमं शीलं समुन्मीलति॥७९॥

One may dive into the waters, he may ascend to the top of mount Meru, he may overcome enemies in a battle, he may devote himself to trade, agriculture, or service etc., he may study all branches of learning and the arts, or he may voyage with great effort through the extensive arial regions, but that which is not to happen in this world, never happens; how can that, which is destined to befall under the influence of fate, be averted?

ऐश्वर्यस्य विभूषणं सुजनता शौर्यस्य वाक्संयमो
ज्ञानस्योपशमः श्रुतस्य विनयो वित्तस्य पात्रे व्ययः।
अक्रोधस्तपसः क्षमा प्रभवितुर्धर्मस्य निर्व्याजता
सर्वेषामपि सर्वकारणमिदं शीलं परं भूषणम्।।८०।।

Good behaviour is the ornament of greatness; silence of valour, restraint sense of learning, humility of knowledge, spending in the right direction of wealth, freedom from anger of austerities; forgiveness of a man in power, and freedom from hypocrisy of religious vows, while good character, which is the root of all these, is the best of all the ornaments.

नेता यस्य बृहस्पतिः प्रहरणं वज्रं सुराः सैनिकाः
स्वर्गो दुर्गमनुग्रहः खलु हरेरैरावतो वाहनम्।
इत्याश्चर्यवलान्वितोऽपि बलभिद्भग्नः परैः संगरे
तद्व्यक्तं ननु दैवमेव शरणं धिग्धिग्वृथा पौरुषम्।।८१।।

Indra was guided by Bṛhaspati and was armed with the thunderbolt, the deities were his soldiers, heaven was his citadel, Airāvata was his elephant; he was undoubtedly the favourite of Hari though he had all this retinue and was endowed with power. Still he was defeated in battle by his enemies. Hence evidently the power of fate is all in all; oh! fie on vain human efforts.

भग्नाशस्य करण्डपीडिततनोर्म्लानेन्द्रियस्य क्षुधा
कृत्वाखुर्विवरं स्वयं निपतितो नक्तं मुखे भोगिनः।
तृप्तस्तत्पिशितेन सत्वरमसौ तेनैव यातः पथा
स्वस्थास्तिष्ठत दैवमेव हि परं वृद्धौ क्षये कारणम्।।८२।।

A mouse, gnawing a hole into a basket, at night, fell into the mouth of a serpent with its body pent up in a basket and its limbs weakened by starvation, had grown despondent. Filled with its meat the serpent quickly glided away through the same hole made by the mouse; see, my men, it is destiny alone which is the cause of the rise and fall of men.

प्रायः कन्दुकपातेनोत्पतत्यार्यः पतन्नपि।
तथा त्वनार्यः पतति मृत्पिण्डपतनं यथा॥८३॥

Though falling, a noble man generally falls like a ball but a mean fellow falls like a lump of clay.

खल्वाटो दिवसेश्वरस्य किरणैः संतापिते मस्तके
वाञ्छन्देशमनातपं द्रुतगतिस्तालस्य मूलं गतः।
तत्राप्यस्य महाफलेन पतता भग्नं सशब्दं शिरः
प्रायो गच्छति यत्र दैवहतकस्तत्रैव यान्त्यापदः॥८४॥

A bald man, scorched on the head by the rays of the sun and wishing for a shady place, went to a palm tree. There, a big fruit falling from the tree, broke his pate with a crash. Verily misfortunes do, indeed, go there where a lucky man goes.

वरं तुङ्गच्छृङ्गाद्गुरुशिखरिणः क्वापि विषमे
पतित्वायं कायः कठिनदृषदन्तर्विदलितः।
वरं न्यस्तो हस्तः फणिपतिमुखे तीव्रदशने
वरं वह्नौ पातस्तदपि न कृतः शीलविलयः॥८५॥

Better to fall from the lofty top of a great mountain in some difficult place and have the body dashed to pieces among hard rock; better to pat the hand in the mouth of a serpent having harp fangs : better to fall into the fire than to swerve from good conduct.

सृजति तावदशेषगुणाकरं
पुरुषरत्नमलंकरणं भुवः।
तदपि तत्क्षणभङ्गि करोति चे-
दह ह कष्टमपण्डितता विधेः॥८६॥

The creator first creates a male jewel, a very mine of all virtues, and an ornament of the world, then in a moment breaks him down. Oh alas! How unreasonable is the action of the creator!

येनैवाम्बरखण्डेन संवितो निशि चन्द्रमाः।
तेनैव च दिवा भानुरहो दौर्गत्यमेतयोः॥८७॥

The sun is covered by day with the same strip of *Ambara* (sky-cloth) with which the moon is covered at night. Oh! the misery of these!

प्रियसख विपद्दण्डाघातप्रवातपरम्परा-
परिचयचले चिन्ताचक्रे निधाय विधिः खलः।
मृदमिव बलात्पिण्डीकृत्य प्रगल्भकुलालव-
द्भ्रमयति मनो नो जानीमः किमत्र विधास्यति॥८८॥

Beloved one! Wicked fate, like a *skilful* potter, per force having rolled our mind into a ball of day, as it were, whirls it round and round by placing it on the wheel of anxiety which revolves being driven by a series of stroken from the rod in the form of adversity; we do not know what fate will do!

विरम विरमायासादस्माद्दुरध्यवसायतो
विपदि महतां धैर्यध्वंसं यदीक्षितुमीहसे।
अयि जडविधे कल्पापायेऽप्यपेतनिजक्रमाः
कुलशिखरिणः क्षुद्रा नैते न वा जलराशयः॥८९॥

Oh idiotic fate, seek you to extinct the boldness of the great people causing them dangers. Leave off this wickedness. See, how stately stand the seas and the mighty mountains at the end of the ages.

दैवेन प्रभुणा स्वयं जगति यद्यस्य प्रमाणीकृतं
तत्तस्योपनमेन्मनागपि महान्नैवाश्रयः कारणम्।
सर्वाशापरिपूरके जलधरे वर्षत्यपि प्रत्यहं
सूक्ष्मा एव पतन्ति चातकमुखे द्वित्राः पयोबिन्दवः॥९०॥

That, which is fixed as one's portion in this world by all-powerful Destiny, will go to him; patronage of the great is not at all the cause of the acquisition. Though the cloud, the gratifier of the desires of all beings, showers daily, only two or three minute drops of water fall into the mouth of a Cātaka bird.

नमस्यामो देवान्ननु हतविधेस्तेऽपि वशगा
विधिर्वन्द्यः सोऽपि प्रतिनियतकर्मैकफलदः।
फलं कर्मायत्तं किममरगणैः किं च विधिना
नमस्तत्कर्मभ्यो विधिरपि न येभ्यः प्रभवति॥९१॥

We shall bow to the gods, but then, even they are subject to the *accursed* fate; fate ought to receive our homage; but even fate dispenses the fruits consistent with each action. The fruit being dependent on action what is (have we to do) with the gods and what is with fate! Bow to those actions, which even fate cannot control.

ब्रह्मा येन कुलालवन्नियमितो ब्रह्माण्डभाण्डोदरे
विष्णुर्येन दशावतारगहने क्षिप्तो महासंकटे।
रुद्रो येन कपालपाणिपुटके भिक्षाटनं सेवते
सूर्यो भ्राम्यति नित्यमेव गगने तस्मै नमः कर्मणे॥९२॥

Adoration to action by which creator has been constrained to work like a potter in the hallow of this universe; Viṣṇu is thrown into the great difficulty of the troublesome ten incarnations, Rudra was forced to wander for a begging with the skull in his joined hands and the Sun was compelled to constantly travel in the heaven.

या साधूंश्च खलान्करोति विदुषो मूर्खान्हितान्द्वेषिणः
प्रत्यक्षं कुरुते परोक्षममृतं हालाहलं तत्क्षणात्।
तामाराधय सत्क्रियां भगवतीं भोक्तुं फलं वाञ्छितं
हे साधो व्यसनैर्गुणेषु विपुलेष्वास्था वृथा मा कृथाः॥९३॥

Oh good man! If you wish to gain your desired objects, do not exert yourself in vain with constant application for the aquisition of various qualifications, but cultivate glorious good conduct which makes evil men good, the fools wise, enemies well-disposed, invisible things visible and turns poison into nectar in a moment.

शुभ्रं सद्म सविभ्रमा युवतयः श्वेतातपत्रोज्ज्वला
लक्ष्मीरित्यनुभूयते चिरमनुस्यूते शुभे कर्मणि।
विच्छिन्ने नितरामनङ्गकलहक्रीडात्रुटत्तन्तुकं
मुक्ताजालमिव प्रयाति झटिति भ्रश्यद्दिशो हश्यताम्॥९४॥

A magnificent mansion, sportive young damsels, prosperity attended with such signs of royalty as the white umbrella are enjoyed by a man as long as he has an unbroken store of merits from his actions in former life; on its being exhausted all these things scatter away in all directions and disappear like the pearls of a necklace whose threads have been broken during love-sports.

गुणवदगुणवद्वा कुर्वता कार्यमादौ
परिणतिरवधार्या यत्नतः पण्डितेन।
अतिरभसकृतानां कर्मणामाविपत्ते-
र्भवति हृदयदाही शल्यतुल्यो विपाकः॥९५॥

A wise man, bent on doing a work, good or bad, should first carefully consider its consequences. An action done in haste becomes, like a dart, poignant to the heart.

स्थाल्यां वैडूर्यमय्यां पचति तिलखलं चान्दनैरिन्धनौघैः
सौवर्णैर्लाङ्गलाग्रैर्विलिखति वसुधामर्कतूलस्य हेतोः।
छित्त्वा कर्पूरखण्डान्वृतिमिह कुरुते कोद्रवाणां समन्ता-
त्प्राप्येमां कर्मभूमिं न चरति मनुजो यस्तपो मन्दभाग्यः॥९६॥

That unfortunate man, who having come into this world of action, does not walk piously, is like one who cooks the less of sesame over fire from fuel consisting largly of sandal wood in a pan of lapis lazuli and is like one who turns the soil with a golden share to get the root of the swallow-wort, or is like one who cuts down a grove of comphor trees to fence in a field of the *Kodrava*.

नैवाकृतिः फलति नैव कुलं न शीलं
विद्यापि नैव न च यत्नकृतापि सेवा।
भाग्यानि पूर्वतपसा खलु संचितानि
काले फलन्ति पुरुषस्य यथैव वृक्षाः॥९७॥

Neither handsome form, nor noble birth nor character, nor

learning, nor even service assiduously performed, but only the merits of men gained by the observance of religious duties in former birth bring forth as a tree bears fruit in its season.

मज्जत्वम्भसि यातु मेरुशिखरं शत्रूञ्जयत्वाहवे
वाणिज्यं कृषिसेवनं च सकला विद्याः कलाः शिक्षतु।
आकाशं विपुलं प्रयातु खगवत्कृत्वा प्रयत्नं परं
नाभाव्यं भवतीह कर्मवशतो भाव्यस्य नाशः कुतः॥९८॥

That which is not to take place, never takes place, nor is a thing fated to take place averted in this world, owing to the force of destiny, though a man may live into water, ascend to the top of the mount Meru, conquer enemies in battle, learn trade, agriculture and all other arts and sciences, and pass like a bird with great effort through the infinite sky.

वने रणे शत्रुजलाग्निमध्ये
महार्णवे पर्वतमस्तके वा।
सुप्तं प्रमत्तं विषमस्थितं वा
रक्षन्ति पुण्यानि पुराकृतानि॥९९॥

The religious merits earned in previous birth save the person from dangers caused in the forests, battles, foes, fire and by a fall from peaks, in seas, in water and when awake or asleep or in distress.

भीमं वनं भवति यस्य पुरं प्रधानं
सर्वो जनः स्वजनतामुपयाति तस्य।
कृत्स्ना च भूर्भवति संनिधिरत्नपूर्णा
यस्यास्ति पूर्वसुकृतं विपुलं नरस्य॥१००॥

For the person who has plenty of merit earned in previous birth, a dangerous forest become his best residence, all people become his good friends, and the earth fills in with all gems and resources.

इति भर्तृहरिविरचितं नीतिशतकं समाप्तम्।

२

श्रृङ्गारशतकम्

शंभुस्वयंभुहरयो हरिणेक्षणानां
येनाक्रियन्त सततं गृहकर्मदासाः।
वाचामगोचरचरित्रविचित्रिताय
तस्मै नमो भगवते मकरध्वजाय॥१॥

Salutation to the great lord Cupid with his fish-flag, by whom the great cosmic rulers like Saṁbhu (Śiva), Svayaṁbhu (Brahmā) and Hari are made the perpetual domestic servants of deer-eyed women and whose great achievements, beggaring description and beyond words cover him with wonderful glory.

स्मितेन भावेन च लज्जया भिया
पराङ्मुखैरर्धकटाक्षवीक्षणैः।
वचोभिरीर्ष्याकलहेन लीलया
समस्तभावैः खलु बन्धनं स्त्रियः॥२॥

By all the love expressions like a smile, a facial love expression, bashfulness, fright, amorous half-glances from aside, sweet-ringing words, jealousy, quarrel, and elegant sportive movements, women bind men by chains.

भ्रूचातुर्यात्कुञ्चिताक्षाः कटाक्षाः
स्निग्धा वाचो लज्जितान्ताश्च हासाः।
लीलामन्दं प्रस्थितं च स्थितं च
स्त्रीणामेतद्भूषणं चायुधं च॥३॥

Significant side-glances with cunning knitting of the eyebrows, whispered words breathing love, laughter closing with exhibition of bashfulness, slow and gay gait and amorously elegant of repose-postures-all these are women's ornaments and also their weapons.

क्वचित्सभ्रूभङ्गैः क्वचिदपि च लज्जापरिगतैः
क्वचिद्भूरित्रस्तैः क्वचिदपि च लीलाविलसितैः।
कुमारीणामेतैर्मदनसुभगैर्नेत्रवलितैः
स्फुरन्नीलाब्जानां प्रकरपरिकीर्णा इव दिशः॥४॥

By the lovely eye-movements of maidens cupid-charged, sometimes coupled with eye-brow knits, with expressions of bashfulness, with tremor, with naive love-betraying graces, the space all round appears as if strewn with clusters of blooming blue lotuses.

वक्त्रं चन्द्रविकासि पङ्कजपरीहासक्षमे लोचने
वर्णः स्वर्णमपाकरिष्णुरलिनीजिष्णुः कचानां चयः।
वक्षोजाविभकुम्भविभ्रमहरौ गुर्वी नितम्बस्थली
वाचां हारि च मार्दवं युवतिषु स्वाभाविकं मण्डनम्॥५॥

Face is lovely like Moon, eyes capable of rediculating lotuses, colour beating the colour of gold, black locks, on the head conquer the black bees hovering near in numbers, breasts lovely like elephants' head, buttocks massive, enchanting sweetness of speech-all these are the natural adornments of maidens.

स्मितं किंचिन्मुग्धं सरलतरलो हष्टिविभवः
परिस्पन्दो वाचामभिनवविलासोक्तिसरसः।
गतानामारम्भः किसलयितलीलापरिकरः
स्पृशन्त्यास्तारुण्यं किमिव न हि रम्यं मृगदृशः॥६॥

Lovely smile with some significance, eye-expressions of combined innocence and love-tinge words issuing from the lips, sweet and significant beginnings of love gaits, the sprouting of tender-youth-graces–what is not charming in a deer-eyed maiden just entering into youth?

द्रष्टव्येषु किमुत्तमं मृगदृशः प्रेमप्रसन्नं मुखं
घ्रातव्येष्वपि किं तदास्यपवनः श्राव्येषु किं तद्वचः।
किं स्वाद्येषु तदोष्ठपल्लवरसः स्पृश्येषु किं तद्वपु-
र्ध्येयं किं नवयौवनं सहृदयैः सर्वत्र तद्विभ्रमाः॥७॥

What is the best of things to see? a deer-eyed maiden's face bright with love. What is the sweetest fragrance to smell? Her mouth-breath. What is the sweetest thing to hear? Her speech. What is sweetest thing to taste? The honey of her rosy lips. Which is the most agreeble to touch? Her body. What is the best to meditate upon for youngmen of tastes? Her budding youth and the resemblances to her appearing everywhere.

एताश्चलद्वलयसंहतिमेखलोत्थ-
झङ्कारनूपुरपराजितराजहंस्यः।
कुर्वन्ति कस्य न मनो विवशं तरुण्यो
वित्रस्तमुग्धहरिणीसदृशैः कटाक्षैः॥८॥

These young swans by the sweet sounds produced by the precious stones on the moving bracelets, waist-belt and anklets whose mind do they not enchant and make captive with their glances lovely like those of young deer in fright and bewilderment?

कुङ्कुमपङ्ककलङ्कितदेहा
गौरपयोधरकम्पितहारा।
नूपुरहंसरणत्पदपद्मा
कं न वशीकुरुते भुवि रामा॥९॥

Whose bodies are smeared with *kesari* paste, whose necklaces move to and fro on their white breasts, with ankelet sounds from their lotus feet calling to mind swans following them, attracted by their lovely gait. Whom in this world do not lovely women captivate?

नूनं हि ते कविवरा विपरीतवाचो
ये नित्यमाहुरबला इति कामिनीस्ताः।
याभिर्विलोलतरतारकदृष्टिपातैः
शक्रादयोऽपि विजितास्त्वबलाः कथं ताः॥१०॥

Surely, all the great poets *do speak* for they always describe lover-maidens as the weaker sex. How can they be weak by whose love glances the great Indra and others are also easily won.

नूनमाज्ञाकरस्तस्याः सुभ्रुवो मकरध्वजः।
यतस्तन्नेत्रसंचारसूचितेषु प्रवर्तते॥११॥

Surely, the cupid is a humble servant of the damsel having lovely eye-brows, because she overpowers the hearts of those who are aimed at by her glances.

केशाः संयमिनः श्रुतेरपि परं पारं गते लोचने
अन्तर्वक्त्रमपि स्वभावशुचिभिः कीर्णं द्विजानां गणैः।
मुक्तानां सतताधिवासरुचिरौ वक्षोजकुम्भाविमा-
वित्थं तन्वि वपुः प्रशान्तमपि ते रागं करोत्येव नः॥१२॥

Oh young women of slender frame! your locks are tied up. (They are described as *saṁyami yogis* with their senses and mind tied up and restrained without being let loose); your eyes reach the border of your ear. (They have reached the shore of the ocean of the Vedic knowledge). The interior of your mouth is full with pure white teeth (*dvijas,* twice born). (It is filled with number of spotlessly pure twice-born men). These elephant-head-like breasts wearing always pearl necklaces are described as being the permanent resting place of Brahman-seer *Muktas* free from the pangs and bonds of *saṁsāra*. In this way, your body, though in a way full of peace, and opposite of agitating passions, rouses in our hearts the deepest passion.

मुग्धे धानुष्कता केयमपूर्वा त्वयि दृश्यते।
यया विध्यसि चेतांसि गुणैरेव न सायकैः॥१३॥

Oh lovely woman! What an extraordinary skill is displayed

by you, you hit the targets of men's hearts by strings only, not by arrows.

सति प्रदीपे सत्यग्नौ सत्सु तारारवीन्दुषु।
विना मे मृगशावाक्ष्या तमोभूतमिदं जगत्॥१४॥

With lights shining, with fire blazing, with stars, sun and moon shining, this world is full of darkness to me without deer-eyed beloved.

उद्वृत्त स्तनभार एव तरले नेत्रे चले भ्रूलते
रागाधिष्ठितमोष्ठपल्लवमिदं कुर्वन्तु नाम व्यथाम्।
सौभाग्याक्षरपङ्क्तिकेव लिखिता पुष्पायुधेन स्वयं
मध्यस्थापि करोति तापमधिकं रोमावलिः केन सा॥१५॥

By all means let her massive breasts trespassing beyond bounds, her ever moving unsteady eyes, her eye-brows often knitting, her tender lips with redness and passion, cause pain in my heart. But why should this row of hairs painted by the hand of flower-armed cupid Himself like a row of luck-indicating letters, loveliest looking, occupying a middle position in the body, produce heat and burning sensation?

मुखेन चन्द्रकान्तेन महानीलैः शिरोरुहैः।
कराभ्यां पद्मरागाभ्यां रेजे रत्नमयीव सा॥१६॥

With face lovely like the Moon (*Candrakānta,* crystal-stone) with *nīla* hairs (black coloured) gems of great value, with palms, red like lotuses (*padmarāga* stones) she shone like full of gems of various kinds.

गुरुणा स्तनभारेण मुखचन्द्रेण भास्वता।
शनैश्चराभ्यां पादाभ्यां रेजे ग्रहमयीव सा॥१७॥

With weighty breasts, with shining of her moon-face, with her legs moving slowly, she shone as full of planets.

तस्याः स्तनौ यदि घनौ जघनं च हारि
वक्त्रं च चारु तव चित्त किमाकुलत्वम्।
पुण्यं कुरुष्व यदि तेषु तवास्ति वाञ्छा
पुण्यैर्विना न हि भवन्ति समीहितार्थाः॥१८॥

If her breasts are massive, buttocks are lovely, and face is beautiful, oh my mind! why are you worried and lost in thought thinking about them? If you want to covet them, earn merit by meritorious acts. This kind of desired objects cannot be obtained without plenty of merit.

इमे तारुण्यश्रीनवपरिमलाः प्रौढसुरत-
प्रतापप्रारम्भाः स्मरविजयदानप्रतिभुवः।
चिरं चेतश्चोरा अभिनवविकारैकगुरवो
विलासव्यापाराः किमपि विजयन्ते मृगदृशाम्॥१९॥

The fresh fragrance and loveliness of budding youth, the commencement of passionate and keen sexual sports, the heart-stealing love-charged graces inflaming the heart with even new passion, guaranteeing victory to cupid-such indescribable charms of deer-eyed women are surpassingly powerful.

प्रणयमधुराः प्रेमोद्गारा रसाश्रयतां गताः
भणितिमृदुला मुग्धप्रायाः प्रकाशितसम्मदाः।
प्रकृतिसुभगा विस्रम्भार्द्राः स्मरोदयदायिनो
रहसि किमपि स्वैरालापा हरन्ति मृगीदृशाम्॥२०॥

The secret love-speeches of deer-eyed women laden with love-sweetness, breathing deep affection, full of deep emotion, softly uttered, moist with sincerity, evoking more and more passion with indescribable power carry away our hearts.

विश्रम्य विश्रम्य वने द्रुमाणां
छायासु तन्वी विचचार काचित्।
स्तनोत्तरीयेण करोद्धृतेन
निवारयन्ती शशिनो मयूखान्॥२१॥

One woman of slender frame wandered resting and resting

under the dark shades of trees warding off the rays of the moon with a breast covering cloth removed therefrom and held by her hand.

अदर्शने दर्शनमात्रकामा
दृष्ट्वा परिष्वङ्गरसैकलोला।
आलिङ्गितायां पुनरायताक्ष्या-
माशास्महे विग्रहयोरभेदम्॥२२॥

When she is not seen, we have desire to see her. Having seen her we desire only for the sweetness of her embrace. When that long-eyed woman is embraced, we keenly wish for the inseparable unity of the two bodies.

मालती शिरसि जृम्भणोन्मुखी
चन्दनं वपुषि कुङ्कुमाविलम्।
वक्षसि प्रियतमा मदालसा
स्वर्ग एष परिशिष्ट आगमः॥२३॥

The *jasmine* garland on her head, the flowers beginning to blow, *keśarī*-mixed sandal-paste just put over the body, the wine-tipsy dearest hugged part in the bosom-all these are real heaven–happiness. The heaven described by the scripture is merely secondary.

प्राङ्मा मेति मनागनागतरसं जाताभिलाषं ततः
सव्रीडं तवनु श्लथीकृततनु प्रत्यस्तधैर्यं पुनः।
प्रेमार्द्रं स्पृहणीयनिर्भररहःक्रीडा प्रगल्भं ततो
निश्शंकाङ्गविकर्षणाधिकसुखं रम्यं कुलस्त्रीरतम्॥२४॥

Delightful is the amour with one's legitimate wife with cries of "no" "no" in the beginning, without exhibition of passion, then desire dawning in the heart, then with bashfulness, then lesser resistence to embraces, lessening of obstimate stiffness, warm affection and love-passion getting the better of her, willing response and even the taking initiative in intimate love sports, then delightful, unreserved hard-pressing embraces with all limbs rapturously co-operating.

उरसि निपतितानां स्रस्तधम्मिल्लकानां
मुकुलितनयनानां किंचिदुन्मीलितानाम्।
उपरि सुरतखेदस्विन्नगण्डस्थलाना-
मधरमधु वधूनां भाग्यवन्तः पिबन्ति॥२५॥

Fortunate men only drink honey of the lips of their sweet-hearts lying over the bosom being tired after their long amorous sports in that posture with their weary cheeks and chin over the men's face when they tie up locks united and scattered dishevelled and eyes closed in sweet ecstasy.

आमीलितनयनानां यः सुरतरसोऽनुसंविदं भाति।
मिथुनैर्मिथोऽवधारितमवितथमिदमेव कामनिर्वहणम्॥२६॥

The sweetness and rapture visibly evident from her eyes closed in the excess of ecstacy the mutually transparent excessive joy enjoyed by both-this alone will show the fullness of sexual delight.

इदमनुचितमक्रमश्च पुंसां
यदिह जरास्वपि मान्मथा विकाराः।
तदपि च न कृतं नितम्बिनीनां
स्तनपतनावधि जीवितं रतं वा॥२७॥

If passion impulses rise in men's hearts even in old age, that is surely improper and inopportune – the same must be said about women in whose case it may be said that either their life or their amours must stop with the falling down of their breasts.

राजंस्तृष्णाम्बुराशेर्नहि जगति गतः कश्चिदेवावसानं
को वार्थोऽर्थैः प्रभूतैः स्ववपुषि गलिते यौवने सानुरागे।
गच्छामः सद्म यावद्विकसितनयनेन्दीवरालोकिनीना-
माक्रम्याक्रम्य रूपं झटिति न जरया लुप्यते प्रेयसीनाम्॥२८॥

Oh King! my master! There is no one who can get to the end of his desires vast like an ocean. What is the good of wealth however great when one's youth which is the time for the satisfaction of sexual love, goes away from his body? We must return to our homes with our sweet-hearts looking forward with eager eyes to our arrival, before their loveliness and beauty are trodden and effaced by the setting in of old age.

रागस्यागारमेकं नरकशतमहादुःखसंप्राप्तिहेतु-
मोहस्योत्पत्तिबीजं जलधरपटलं ज्ञानताराधिपस्य।
कन्दर्पस्यैकमित्रं प्रकटितविविधस्पष्टदोषप्रबन्धं
लोकेऽस्मिन्न ह्यनर्थव्रजकुलभवनं यौवनादन्यदस्ति॥२९॥

In this world, there is nothing so bad as youth which gives birth to countless difficulties, is an abode of unhealthy passions, source of many great miseries equal to a hundred hells; progenitor of delusions, cluster of thick clouds obscuring the moon of the intelligence, a best friend of cupid and which generates and unfolds more and more unhealthy desires.

शृङ्गारद्रुमनीरदे प्रसृमरक्रीडारसस्त्रोतसि
प्रद्युम्नप्रियबान्धवे चतुरवाङ्मुक्ताफलोदन्वति।
तन्वीनेत्रचकोरपार्वणविधौ सौभाग्यलक्ष्मीनिधौ
धन्यः कोऽपि न विक्रियां कलयते प्राप्ते नवे यौवने॥३०॥

He is a rare great man of good fortune whose heart is undisturbed by passions on the setting in of fresh youth which is a rain-pouring cloud of the tree of sexual love, a flowing stream of passionate desire for love-sports, the dear friend of cupid, an ocean teeming with pearl-like, fine and clever language, the full-moon with rays sipped eagerly by the chakora-like eyes of young women of slender face and the veritable mind of loveliness and glory.

संसारेऽस्मिन्नसारे कुनृपतिभवनद्वारसेवाकलङ्क-
व्यासङ्गव्यस्तधैर्यं कथममलधियो मानसं सन्निदध्युः।
यद्येताः प्रोद्यदिन्दुद्युतिनिचयभृतो न स्युरम्भोजनेत्राः
प्रेङ्खत्काञ्चीकलापाः स्तनभरविनमन्मध्यभाजस्तरुण्यः॥३१॥

How would the noble men of pure hearts set their hearts on this wretched wordly life *'saṁsāra'* in which livelihood has to be eked out by waiting in service at the door of unworthy kings?

Were it not for the passion for pleasures with these young girls shining with the splendour of the rising moon, eyes lovely like lotuses, the gold belts ringing with the sound of gold beads and with bare waists threatening to break under the burden of heavy breasts.

सिद्धाध्यासितकन्दरे हरवृषस्कन्धावरुग्णद्रुमे
गङ्गाधौतशिलातले हिमवतः सानौ स्थिते श्रेयसि।
कः कुर्वीत शिरः प्रणाममलिनं ग्लानं मनस्वी जनो
यद्वित्रस्तकुरङ्गशावनयना न स्युः स्मरास्त्रं स्त्रियः॥३२॥

When there is the soul-elevating Himālayan peak with caves inhabited by *Siddhas*, with trees whose branches are broken by the rubbing of 'Śiva's bull's shoulder, with its rocks dashed against by the Gangetic waters (where he may retire and make lovely penance) which thinking man would dishonour his head by bending it before unworthy lords, were it not for women, with eyes like frightened little deer's, pierecing their hearts as sharp arrows.

संसार तव पर्यन्तपदवी न दवीयसी।
अन्तरा दुस्तरा न स्युर्यदि ते मदिरेक्षणाः॥३३॥

Oh world! Worldly material life! Your end will not be long were it not for the intervening women with lovely rolling eyes whose power is difficult to resist.

दिश वनहरिणीभ्यो वंशकाण्डच्छवीनां
कवलमुपलकोटिच्छिन्नमूलं कुशानाम्।
शकयुवतिकपोला पाण्डुताम्बूलवल्ली-
दलमरुणनखाग्रैः पाटितं वा वधूभ्यः॥३४॥

Either give a cud of *Kuśa* grass cut with the sharpedge of stones and green like bamboo leaves to the forest deer or give to young women betel leaves white like the cheeks of *Śaka* young ladies torn in the middle by your reddish nail tips.

असाराः सन्त्वेते विरतिविरसा वादविषया
जुगुप्स्यन्तां यद्वा ननु सकलदोषास्पदमिति।
तथाऽप्येतद्भूमौ न हि परहितात्पुण्यमधिकं
न चास्मिन् संसारे कुवलयदृशो रम्यमपरम्॥३५॥

Be the objects of sensuous pleasures valueless and becoming bitter just at the close of the indulgence, be they discarded as disgusting because of their being attended by ever so many evil consequences. Be that as it may, in this world, there is no greater virtue in doing good to others, nor is there anything more lovely in this worldly life than women whose eyes are like blue lilies.

मात्सर्यमुत्सार्य विचार्य कार्य–
मार्याः समर्यादमिदं वदन्तु।
सेव्या नितम्बाः किमु भूधराणा–
मुत स्मरस्मेरविलासिनीनाम्॥३६॥

Oh Great men! Casting off all prejudices ponder over and tell us for certain without going beyond the bounds of propriety, "which should we seek and take shelter under the sides of mountains or the buttocks of women with deep passion by the impetuous cupid."

संसारे स्वप्नसारे परिणतितरले द्वे गती पण्डितानां
तत्त्वज्ञानामृतौघप्लवललितधियां यातु कालः कथञ्चित्।
नोचेन्मुग्धाङ्गनानां स्तनजघनघनाभोगसंभोगिनीनां
स्थूलोपस्थस्थलीषु स्थगितकरतलस्पर्शलीलोद्यमानाम्॥३७॥

In this worldly life *"Saṁsāra"* fleeting and short lived like a dream shows but bitter consequences there are only two ways for wise. Let their life be spent happily sporting in the nectar's sweet streams of Brahmic knowledge and enjoyment; or else let it be spent in the company of lovely damsels who hug and embrace them in their extensive breasts and buttocks putting their palms over the limbs of their body gently and pleasingly.

आवासः क्रियतां गाङ्गे पापहारिणि वारिणि।
स्तनद्वये तरुण्या वा मनोहारिणि हारिणि॥३८॥

Let a person rest on the banks of the holy Gaṅgā which will remove all his sins or with the lovely and heart-stealing breasts of the young woman.

किमिह बहुभिरुक्तैर्युक्तिशून्यैः प्रलापै-
र्द्वयमिह पुरुषाणां सर्वदा सेवनीयम्।
अभिनवमदलीलालालसं सुन्दरीणां
स्तनभरपरिखिन्नं यौवनं वा वनं वा॥३९॥

Why do you waste words at length in irrational talks like this. The alternative for men to spend their life time is between the youth of beautiful women keenly intent on sexual sports under the excitement of new wine and passed under the heavy weight of massive breasts or the lonely forest–shade.

सत्यं जना वच्मि न पक्षपाताल्लोकेषु सप्तस्वपि तथ्यमेतत्।
नान्यन्मनोहारि नितम्बिनीभ्यो दुःखैकहेतुर्न च कश्चिदन्यः॥४०॥

Oh men in the world! I speak truly to you not out of any partiality. In all the seven worlds this truth holds good. There is nothing so lovely and pleasing as a woman with massive buttocks nor is there anything productive of so much misery as woman.

कान्तेत्युत्पललोचनेति विपुलश्रोणीभरेत्युन्नम-
त्पीनोत्तुङ्गपयोधरेति सुमुखाम्भोजेति सुभ्रूरिति।
दृष्ट्वा माद्यति मोदतेऽभिरमते प्रस्तौति विद्वानपि
प्रत्यक्षाशुचिभस्त्रिकां स्त्रियमहो मोहस्य दुश्चेष्टितम्॥४१॥

Even a man of learning loses himself, gets overjoyed and mightily pleased and begins to describe woman's flesh which is on its face a bundle of unclean, awkward and nauseous things as admiringly as my love! With eyes black like a lily, with buttocks extensive, with breasts stout and high spread above the bosom, with lotuse-like lovely face, fine eye-brows, what dire effects are produced by false illusions!

स्मृता भवति तापाय दृष्टा चोन्मादकारिणी।
स्पृष्टा भवति मोहाय सा नाम दयिता कथम्॥४२॥

If she is remembered, she produces love-fever, if she is seen she clouds the senses; if touched she stupifies. How can she be said to be a dear-love.

तावदेवामृतमयी यावल्लोचनगोचरा।
चतुष्पथादतीता तु विषादप्यतिरिच्यते॥४३॥

She is full of nectar only as long as she is in sight. Gone out of sight beyond the function of roads, she burns the lover more than deadly poison.

नामृतं न विषं किञ्चिदेतां मुक्त्वा नितम्बिनीम्।
सैवामृतलता रक्ता विरक्ता विषवल्लरी॥४४॥

Expecting this woman of big buttocks there is neither any other nectar nor other poison. If in company, she is an ambrosia. If separated she is a poisonous creeper.

आवर्तः संशयानामविनयभवनं पट्टणं साहसानां
दोषाणां सन्निधानं कपटशतमयं क्षेत्रमप्रत्ययानाम्।
स्वर्गद्वारस्य विघ्नो नरकपुरमुखं सर्वमायाकरण्डं
स्त्रीयन्त्रं केन सृष्टं विषममृतमयं प्राणिलोकस्य पाशः॥४५॥

The trap of woman is a whirlpool of doubts, a home of breaches of discipline, a crowded city of devil-daring adventures, a big group of faults, a land of hundreds of cunning deceits, a bar to entry into *svarga*, a city of Hell, a receptacle of all cunning and dissembling who has created this trap of woman, which is the nectar-sweet-seeming poison and a binding fetter for men.

नो सत्येन मृगाङ्क एष वदनीभूतो न चेन्दीवर–
द्वन्द्वं लोचनतां गतं न कनकैरप्यङ्गयष्टिः कृताः।
किं त्वेवं कविभिः प्रतारितमनास्तत्त्वं विजानन्नपि
त्वङ्मांसास्थिमयं वपुर्मृगदृशां मन्दो जनः सेवते॥४६॥

This Moon in the sky has not really become this woman's

face nor have two black lilies taken the shape of her eyes. Nor is her slender body made of gold. She is falsely described thus by poets deceived by whose words even sober men become fools and run after them and dote on woman's body of skin, flesh and bone.

लीलावतीनां सहजा विलासास्त एव मूढस्य हृदि स्फुरन्ति।
रागो नलिन्या हि निसर्गसिद्धस्तत्र भ्रमत्येव मुधा षडङ्घ्रिः॥४७॥

The lovely graces of women's glance, gait and other movements, are natural to them, not at all prompted by any love for this fool in whose mind they loom largely as indications of love to him. The reddish hue (*Rāga*, love) of lotus is natural to them but the honey-bee whirls round and round about them foolishly mistaking the *Rāga* as love for it.

यदेतत्पूर्णेन्दुद्युतिहरमुदाराकृतिधरं
मुखाब्जं तन्वङ्ग्याः किल वसति यत्राधरमधु।
इदं तत्किंपाकद्रुमफलमिदानीमतिरसं
व्यतीतेऽस्मिन् काले विषमिव भविष्यत्यसुखदम्॥४८॥

This face of the woman of slender frame which excels the loveliness of the full Moon and very beautiful in which honey is stored in the lips, and is full of exceeding sweetness now like a fruit of a tree, will become bitter and unpleasant like poison after this season of beauty is gone.

उन्मीलत्त्रिवलीतरङ्गनिलया प्रोत्तुङ्गपीनस्तन-
द्वन्द्वेनोद्धतचक्रवाकयुगला वक्राम्बुजोद्भासिनी।
कान्ताकारधरा नदीयमभितः क्रूरात्र नापेक्षते
संसारार्णवमज्जनं यदि तदा दूरेण सन्त्यज्यताम्॥४९॥

If you do not wish to plunge into the ocean of world, stand far away from this river of woman with the triple row of hairs near the naval whose charms whirl like a whirlpool, with her two breasts high and stout, looking like a pair of cakravāka birds sitting on the river sand, with her face lovely like a lotus in the river, having a very lovely appearance but with a cruel heart within.

जल्पन्ति सार्धमन्येन पश्यन्त्यन्यं सविभ्रमाः।
हृद्गतं चिन्तयन्त्यन्यं प्रियः को नाम योषिताम्॥५०॥

They talk amorously with one, cast loving glances on other; cherish in their heart yet another. Who is really dear to women?

मधु तिष्ठति वाचि योषितां हृदि हालाहलमेव केवलम्।
अत एव निपीयतेऽधरो हृदयं मुष्टिभिरेव ताड्यते॥५१॥

Honey exists in the mouth of women. But there is bitter poison only in their heart. For this reason their lip is sucked, but heart is slapped with the wrist.

अपसर सखे दूरादस्मात्कटाक्षविषानला-
त्प्रकृतिविषमाद्योषित्सर्पाद्विलासफणाभृतः।
इतरफणिना दष्टः शक्यश्चिकित्सितुमौषधै-
श्चतुरवनिताभोगिग्रस्तं त्यजन्ति हि मन्त्रिणः॥५२॥

Oh my friend! Move away from the blazing fire of the glances of women, from the naturally crooked poisonous serpent called woman with hoods spread in the shape of sporting graces. A man bitten by other serpents can be cured of the poison by the medicines. *Māntrika* yogis (who can save from serpent poison) give up as hopeless the attempt to rid a person of love-poison injected by a clever woman.

विस्तारितं मकरकेतनधीवरेण
स्त्रीसंज्ञितं वडिशमत्र भवाम्बुराशौ।
येनाचिरात्तदधरामिषलोलमर्त्य-
मत्स्यान्विकृष्य विपचत्यनुरागवह्नौ॥५३॥

The fisherman Cupid of fish-flag casts wide net in the ocean of world with a bait called woman by means of which he very quickly draws into his net the men hankering after the flesh of her lips like fish and fry them in the fire of love-sickness.

कामिनीकायकान्तारे कुचपर्वतदुर्गमे।
मा सञ्चर मनःपान्थ तत्रास्ते स्मरतस्करः॥५४॥

Oh my mind-traveller! Do not wander in the dreary forest

of a woman's body with inaccessible mountain like breasts, there is a cupid-robber.

व्यादीर्घेण चलेन वक्रगतिना तेजस्विना भोगिना
नीलाब्जद्युतिवाहिना वरमहं दष्टो न तच्चक्षुषा।
दष्टस्सन्ति चिकित्सका दिशि दिशि प्रायेण धर्मार्थिनो
मुग्धाक्षीक्षणवीक्षितस्य न हि मे वैद्यो न वाप्यौषधम्॥५५॥

I would rather be bitten by a long crookedly crawling serpent of beautiful, dark colour with virulent poison, than be amorously looked at by a woman having all these qualities. There are good and clever physicians doing rescue work all over the world but there is not a single physician or medicine that can heal me, who is entrapped by a momentary glance of a beautiful woman.

इह हि मधुरगीतं नृत्तमेतद्रसोऽयं
स्फुरति परिमलोऽसौ स्पर्श एव स्तनानाम्।
इति हतपरमार्थैरिन्द्रियैर्भ्राम्यमाणः
स्वहितकरणधूर्तैः पञ्चभिर्वञ्चितोऽस्मि॥५६॥

Alas! I had been fooled and deceived by five rogues- senses posing as my friends and well-wishers but really "deluded me holding out false and untrue temptations saying here is sweet music, here is sweet dancing, here is a sweet drink, here is sweet fragrance, these breasts give the sweetest touch."

न गम्यो मन्त्राणां न च भवति भैषज्यविषयो
न चापि प्रध्वंसं व्रजति विविधैः शान्तिकशतैः।
भ्रमावेशादङ्गे किमपि विदधद्भङ्गमसकृत्
स्मरापस्मारोऽयं भ्रमयति दृशं घूर्णयति च॥५७॥

Love-sickness which paralyses consciousness is neither curable by *mantra*-incantations nor by medicine nor does it end by hundreds of various healing vedic *Śānti* rites. By producing feeling both of mind and body, it often disables the limbs and makes the eyes look wild and the head giddy.

जात्यन्धाय च दुर्मुखाय च जराजीर्णाखिलाङ्गाय च
ग्रामीणाय च दुष्कुलाय च गलत्कुष्ठाभिभूताय च।
यच्छन्तीषु मनोहरं निजवपुर्लक्ष्मीलवश्रद्धया
पण्यस्त्रीषु विवेककल्पलतिकाशस्त्रीषु रज्येत कः॥५८॥

Who could conceive any attachment for courtesans selling their beautiful bodies for little money like commercial goods to the congenital blind? The ugly, decrepit old men with all limbs worn out by age, the village rustic, the man of disreputable birth, the ulcerous lepper.

वेश्यासौ मदनज्वाला रूपेन्धनसमेधिता।
कामिभिर्यत्र हूयन्ते यौवनानि धनानि च॥५९॥

This courtesan is a love-fire flaming with the fuel of beauty in which the youth and wealth of amorous young men are thrown as offerings.

कश्चुम्बति कुलपुरुषो वेश्याधरपल्लवं मनोज्ञमपि।
चारभटचोरचेटकनटविटनिष्ठीवनशरावम्॥६०॥

Which man of good birth could kiss a courtesan's tender lip however lovely which is a spit-receptacle for whores, soldiers, thieves, pimps, actors, charlatans.

धन्यास्त एव धवलायतलोचनानां
तारुण्यदर्पघनपीनपयोधराणाम्।
क्षामोदरोपरि लसत्त्रिवलीलतानां
दृष्ट्वाऽऽकृतिं विकृतमेति मनो न येषाम्॥६१॥

Those only are praise-worthy whose mind is untempted by attractive beautiful women with long bright eyes, stout breasts, proud with youth and the three hair-rows looking like creepers over the slender waists.

बाले लीलामुकुलितममी मन्थरा दृष्टिपाताः
किं क्षिप्यन्ते विरम विरम व्यर्थ एष श्रमस्ते।
सम्प्रत्यन्ये वयमुपरतं बाल्यमास्था वनान्ते
क्षीणो मोहस्तृणमिव जगज्जालमालोकयामः॥६२॥

Oh young girl! stop! stop! Why are you throwing away

your slow eye-glances, half-closed in love! Your pains will be thrown away in vain. We are now entirely a new set of persons. Our youth is gone. We long for the woods. Our love frenzy is all dry. We look upon the world and its temptations as a straw.

इयं बाला मां प्रत्यनवरतमिन्दीवरदल-
प्रभाचोरं चक्षुः क्षिपति किमभिप्रेतमनया।
गतो मोहोऽस्माकं स्मरकुसुमबाणव्यतिकर-
ज्वरज्वाला शान्ता तदपि न वराकी विरमति॥६३॥

This young woman unceasingly casts at me her glances which have stolen the beauty of the blue lotus-leaf. What does she mean? Our infatuation has gone and the burning of the fever produced by contact of the flowery arrows of cupid has been cooled, yet the poor girl does not cease.

रे कन्दर्प करं कदर्थयसि किं कोदण्डटङ्कारितै
रे रे कोकिल कोमलैः कलरवैः किं वा वृथा जल्पसि।
मुग्धे स्निग्धविदग्धमुग्धमधुरैर्लोलैः कटाक्षैरलं
चेतश्चुम्बितचन्द्रचूडचरणध्यानामृतं वर्तते॥६४॥

Oh Cupid! Why are you troubling your arm with the drawing noise of your bow? Oh cuckoo! Why are you cooing in vain your melodian indistinct cries? O lovely girl! Enough with your love-laden, clever, fine, sweet glances. I am now immersed in the nectar like sweet meditation on the feet of the crescent headed Lord, kissed by my mind.

विरहेऽपि सङ्गमः खलु परस्परं सङ्गतं मनो येषाम्।
हृदयमपि विघटितं चेत् सङ्गमे विरहं विशेषयति॥६५॥

If the minds of the couple are united in love, even when there is bodily separation on account of distance and absence, they maybe said to be in union and not separate. If there is mental aversion to each other or even on one side, physical contact will only generate immediate wish for separation.

किं गतेन यदि सा न जीवति
प्राणिति प्रियतमा तथापि किम्।
इत्युदीक्ष्य नवमेघमालिकां
न प्रयाति पथिकः स्वमन्दिरम्॥६६॥

"What is the good of my joining my home?" On seeing these clouds my dearest either has breathed her last in despair or lives with courage. In the first case it is not good to go there after her death. In the second case also it is not good, for her continuing to live betrays 'not enough' love.

विरमत बुधा योषित्सङ्गात्सुखात्क्षणभङ्गुरा-
त्कुरुत करुणामैत्रीप्रज्ञावधूजनसङ्गमम्।
न खलु नरके हाराक्रान्तं घनस्तनमण्डलं
शरणमथवा श्रोणीबिम्बं रणन्मणिमेखलम्॥६७॥

Oh wise men! Desist from association with women and the momentary pleasure derivable therefrom, vanishing quickly. Put your mind in constant touch with compassion for the distressed and affection and love to good men. Substituting, the company of these two for the company of women. Neither the massive breasts of women with hanging necklaces nor their buttocks resounding with the noise of the waist-string beads, will come to your rescue when you will suffer in hell.

यदा योगाभ्यासव्यसनकृशयोरात्ममनसो-
रविच्छिन्ना मैत्री स्फुरति कृतिनस्तस्य किमु तैः।
प्रियाणामालापैरधरमधुभिर्वक्त्रविधुभिः
सनिःश्वासामोदैः सकुचकलशाश्लेषसुरतैः॥६८॥

When the unison between the soul and mind arises by practice of yogic exercise, the lovely speeches, nectar on lips, incence of respiration and coition embracing paps are useless for that person.

यदासीदज्ञानं स्मरतिमिरसञ्चारजनितं
तदा दृष्टं नारीमयमिदमशेषं जगदिति।
इदानीमस्माकं पटुतरविवेकाञ्जनजुषां
समीभूता दृष्टिस्त्रिभुवनमपि ब्रह्म मनुते॥६९॥

When there was darkness of ignorance produced by the shades of night ushered by cupid, the whole world was looked to us as filled with women. Now, when I have been cured of all love-maladies by the application of the medicinal ointment of firm spiritual wisdom, my eyes, attaining the standard of spiritual level, see the three whole worlds as *Brahman*.

तावदेव कृतिनामपि स्फुरत्येष निर्मलविवेकदीपकः।
यावदेव न कुरङ्गचक्षुषां ताड्यते चटुललोचनाञ्चलैः॥७०॥

This spiritual lamp of pure light shines in the minds of strong men only until the pure lamp light is tossed and shaken and extinguished by the glow of amourous glances of deer-eyed women.

वचसि भवति सङ्गत्यागमुद्दिश्य वार्ता
श्रुतिमुखरमुखानां केवलं पण्डितानाम्।
जघनमरुणरत्नग्रन्थिकाञ्चीकलापं
कुवलयनयनानां को विहातुं समर्थः॥७१॥

Even among men learned in the Vedas and frequently engaged in reciting them there arises a mere pious talk of giving up attachments for women. Who has got the strength to part from the buttocks of black-lily-eyed women with the lustre of red-stones in the waist–string ornament?

स्वपरप्रतारकोऽसौ निन्दति योऽलीकपण्डितो युवतीः।
यस्मात्तपसोऽपि फलं स्वर्गः स्वर्गेऽपि चाप्सरसः॥७२॥

He is a false man of learning who despises young girls. He cheats himself and others by doing so because the fruit of '*tapas*' is the heaven where there are celestial nymphs.

मत्तेभकुम्भदलने भुवि सन्ति धीराः
केचित्प्रचण्डमृगराजवधेऽपि दक्षाः।
किन्तु ब्रवीमि बलिनां पुरतः प्रसह्य
कन्दर्पदर्पदलने विरला मनुष्याः॥७३॥

There are valiant men who can break the heads of wild elephants; there are some who are clever in killing even savage lions in a duel, but verily do I say unto you boldly in the presence of brave men, that the men who can conquer proud cupid, are extremely rare.

सन्मार्गे तावदास्ते प्रभवति पुरुषस्तावदेवेन्द्रियाणां
लज्जां तावद्विधत्ते विनयमपि समालम्बते तावदेव।
भ्रूचापाकृष्टमुक्ताः श्रवणपथगता नीलपक्ष्माण एते
यावल्लीलावतीनां हृदि न धृतिमुषो दृष्टिबाणाः
पतन्ति॥७४॥

A man can be in the right path, keep his senses under control and his sense of shame and modesty, only till the over-whelmingly, powerful arrows of amorous young women's glances darting from cupid's bow *i.e.,* their eye-brows, bent and drawn up to the ears with black eye-lids serving as wings, fall over and hit at the target of mind.

उन्मत्तप्रेमसंरम्भादारभन्ते यदङ्गनाः।
तत्र प्रत्यूहमाधातुं ब्रह्मापि खलु कातरः॥७५॥

When young women excitedly begin their love-sports in the heat of their love, even Brahmā would be afraid of throwing obstacles on their way.

तावन्महत्त्वं पाण्डित्यं कुलीनत्वं विवेकिता।
यावज्ज्वलति नाङ्गेषु हतः पञ्चेषुपावकः॥७६॥

Greatness, learning, high birth and wisdom will avail a man as long as the cursed love fire or cupid with his five arrows does not begin to consume him and his limbs.

शास्त्रज्ञोऽपि प्रगुणितनयोऽप्यात्तबोधोऽपि बाढं
संसारेऽस्मिन्भवति विरलो भाजनं सद्गतीनाम्।
येनैतस्मिन्निरयनगरद्वारमुद्घाटयन्ती
वामाक्षीणां भवति कुटिला भ्रूलता कुञ्चिकेव॥७७॥

Even a person well-read in sciences, a master of moral sciences, law and of mature wisdom, does not ordinarily in this world make himself eligible for the attainment of good-worlds because the crooked eye-brows of women of lovely eyes, serve as the key to open the gate-door of the city of hell to him.

कृशः काणः खञ्जः श्रवणरहितः पुच्छविकलो
व्रणी पूयक्लिन्नः कृमिकुलशतैरावृततनुः।
क्षुधाक्षामो जीर्णः पिठरककपालार्पितगलः
शुनीमन्वेति श्वा हतमपि च हन्त्येव मदनः॥७८॥

A dog emaciated, blind of one eye, lame of leg, with ulcers all over the body, blood with puss, with swarms of insects, flies, ants etc. sitting on the wounds starving and hungry, decrepit and old with broken pot hung round the neck, madly goes after the bitch. Cupid does not hesitate to strike to him even.

स्त्रीमुद्रां कुसुमायुधस्य परमां सर्वार्थसम्पत्करी
ये मूढाः प्रविहाय यान्ति कुधियो मिथ्याफलान्वेषिणः।
ते तेनैव निहत्य निर्दयतरं नग्नीकृता मुण्डिताः
केचित्पञ्चशिखीकृताश्च जटिलाः कापालिकाश्चापरे॥७९॥

Those unwise men who give up the fair sex, the favourites of cupid and the givers of all pleasures one could wish for and tread the path of celebrated recluses are mercilessly punished by cupid in that they are made either nude or bare-headed with hairs wholly shaven or the five *tags* of hair or with braided hair or mendicants begging food with pieces of broken pots in hand.

विश्वामित्रपराशरप्रभृतयो वामाम्बुपर्णाशना-
स्तेऽपि स्त्रीमुखपङ्कजं सुललितं दृष्ट्वैव मोहं गताः।
शाल्यन्नं सघृतं पयो दधियुतं ये भुञ्जते मानवा-
स्तेषामिन्द्रियनिग्रहो यदि भवेद्विन्ध्यः प्लवेत्सागरे॥८०॥

The great sages like Viśvāmitra and Parāśara living on air,

water and the leaves of trees even have been driven into love frenzies by merely looking at the lovely lotus–face of women. If men nourished with *stable* rice-food with plenty of ghee, milk and curds, could keep their senses under control the Vindhya mountain will then float over the sea.

परिमलभृतो वाताः शाखा नवाङ्कुरकोटयो
मधुरविधुरोत्कण्ठाभाजः प्रिया पिकपक्षिणाम्।
विरलविरलस्वेदोद्गारा वधूवदनेन्दवः
प्रसरति मधौ धात्र्यां जातो न कस्य गुणोदयः॥८१॥

Gentle winds! Waft the fragrance of blooming flowers, the branches of trees are lovely with tender leaves sprouting; female cuckoos are brimful with sweet passion for their mates. The moon-like faces of young women are decked here and there with (pearl-like) drops of perspiration. When the spring season sets in what on the earth does not gain in loveliness and beauty?

मधुरयं मधुरैरपि कोकिला-
कलरवैर्मलयस्य च वायुभिः।
विरहिणः प्रहिणस्ति शरीरिणो
विपदि हन्त सुधापि विषायते॥८२॥

This spring season causes pain to separated lovers with the amorous indistinct sweet *coos* of female cuckoos, and the Southern Malaya breeze. Alas! When misfortune comes, even nectar becomes bitter and dangerous like pioson.

आवासः किलकिंचितस्य दयिताः पार्श्वे विलासालसाः
कर्णे कोकिलकामिनीकलरवः स्मेरो लतामण्डपः।
गोष्ठी सत्कविभिः समं कतिपयैर्मुग्धाः सितांशोः कराः
केषांचित्सुखयन्नि चात्र हृदयं चैत्रे विचित्राः क्षपाः॥८३॥

The wonderfully beautiful nights of Caitra month fill the heart of some lucky men with delight. What with dear young women full of zest for amorous love sports and slow elegant movements, sweet love-coos of female cuckoos, ringing in the ear, green creeper bowers with flowers, the company of poets singing love songs, the lovely rays of the moon.

पान्थस्त्री विरहानलाहुतिकलामातन्वती मञ्जरी
माकन्देषु पिकाङ्गनाभिरधुना सोत्कण्ठमालोक्यते।
अल्पास्ते नवपाटलापरिमलप्राग्भारपाटच्चरा
वान्ति कान्तिवितानतानवकृतः श्रीखण्डशैलानिलाः॥८४॥

Clusters of flowers look like blazing fire into which hearts of women separated from their lovers gone out as travellers to distant countries are thrown as oblations as it were. Female cuckoos look with keen desire at the mango-tree. The southern breezes from the Malaya hills with sandal wood forests, charged with the fragrance stolen from the young petals of flowers, blow gently relieving the fatigue and warmness in the sultry day.

प्रथितः प्रणयवतीनां तावत्पदमातनोतु हृदि मानः।
भवति न यावच्चन्दनतरुसुरभिर्मलयपवमानः॥८५॥

The unbending pride of the young women, resiting the approaches by their lovers can continue only till the Malaya breezes begin to blow with sandal wood fragrance.

सहकारकुसुमकेसरनिकरभरामोदमूर्च्छितदिगन्ते।
मधुरमधुविधुरमधुपे मधौ भवेत्कस्य नोत्कण्ठा॥८६॥

Who would not become love-sick in the spring when the atmosphere is all round charged with the fragrance of tender mango leaves and flowers and the bees are intoxicated with sweet honey?

अच्छाच्छचन्दनरसार्द्रकरा मृगाक्ष्यो
धारागृहाणि कुसुमानि च कौमुदी च।
मन्दो मरुत्सुमनसः शुचि हर्म्यपृष्ठं
ग्रीष्मे मदं च मदनं च विवर्धयन्ति॥८७॥

In summer, deer-eyed women freshly smeared with purest sandal paste, cool-rooms with water sprays, fine flowers, moon-light, gentle breeze, jasmine flowers, clean upper storey floor, inflame both cupid and love-frenzy or passion.

स्रजो हृद्यामोदा व्यजनपवनश्चन्द्रकिरणाः
परागः कासारो मलयजरजः शीधु विशदम्।
शुचिः सौधोत्सङ्गः प्रतनु वसनं पङ्कजदृशो
निदाघार्तावेतन्सुखमुपलभन्ते सुकृतिनः॥८८॥

In the scorching summer, fortunate men get the pleasure of garlands of sweet fragrance, cool air moved by fans, cool rays of the moon, flower dust, water ponds, the fine of malaya-breezes, pure wine, clean upper storey floor, the thinest dress and lotus eyed women.

सुधाशुभ्रं धाम स्फुरदमलरश्मिः शशधरः
प्रियावक्त्राम्भोजं मलयजरजश्चातिसुरभिः।
स्रजो हृद्यामोदास्तदिदमखिलं रागिणि जने
करोत्यन्तःक्षोभं न तु विषयसंसर्गविमुखे॥८९॥

Clean and white washed houses, Moon-shining brightly, the lotus face of the beloved, the very fragrant Malaya-blown-breeze, fine-dust, sweet smelling garlands,–all these cause agitation in the hearts of lovers, not in the austere man scorning the pleasure of the senses.

तरुणीवेषोद्दीपितकामा विकसज्जातीपुष्पसुगन्धिः।
उन्नतपीनपयोधरभारा प्रावृट् तनुते कस्य न हर्षम्॥९०॥

Whom does not the rainy season delight comparable as it is with a young woman inflaming with love-passions, sweet smelling with blooming jasmine flowers and filled with heavy clouds (breasts high and massive).

वियदुपचितमेघं भूमयः कन्दलिन्यो
नवकुटजकदम्बामोदिनो गन्धवाहाः।
शिखिकुलकलकेकारावरम्या वनान्ताः
सुखिनमसुखिनं वा सर्वमुत्कण्ठयन्ति॥९१॥

The sky thickly covered with clouds, the earth filled with shooting sprouts, the winds carrying the fragrance got from fresh jasmine flowers, gardens resounding with the sweet cries of peacocks, always fill with love longings, men, whether separated from their beloved or in company with them.

उपरि घनं घनपटलं तिर्यग्गिरयोऽपि नर्तितमयूराः
क्षितिरपि कन्दलधवला दृष्टिं पथिकः क्व पातयति॥९२॥

Up above there are numerous thick clouds. On all sides there are peacocks made to dance with joy on hills by the sight of the clouds. The earth is teeming with young tender plants sprouting. Where could the poor traveller safely cast his eyes upon?

इतो विद्युद्वल्ली विलसितमितः केतकितरोः
स्फुरद्गन्धः प्रोद्यज्जलदनिनदस्फूर्जितमितः।
इतः केकीक्रीडाकलकलरवैः पक्ष्मलदृशां
कथं यास्यन्त्येते विरहदिवसाः सम्भृतरसाः॥९३॥

Here are the lightening streets flashing with the fragrance of 'ketakī' flowers, here are the thundering noises of the clouds gathering in the sky; here are the indistinct cries of playing peacocks. How can the days of separation from their lovers be passed easily and pleasantly by women of lovely eye-lids.

असूचीसंचारे तमसि नभसि प्रौढजलद-
ध्वनिप्राज्ञंमन्ये पतति पृषतानां च निचये।
इदं सौदामिन्याः कनककमनीयं विलसितं
मुदं च म्लानिं च प्रथयति पथि स्वैरसुदृशाम्॥९४॥

When the night is pitch dark, the darkness being intense so as not to allow even a pin to move within it, when rain is falling thickly from the clouds, proudly creating noise with their thunder, these lovely gold-cover coloured flashes of lightening fill the hearts of ladies voluntarily seeking their lover's residence by walking in the streets in the nights alternately with joy and sorrow.

आसारेण न हर्म्यतः प्रियतमैर्यातुं बहिः शक्यते
शीतोत्कम्पनिमित्तमायतदृशा गाढं समालिङ्ग्यते।
जाताः शीकरशीतलाश्च मरुतो रत्यन्तखेदच्छिदो
धन्यानां बत दुर्दिनं सुदिनतां याति प्रियासङ्गमे॥९५॥

It is not possible for women to go out of their mansions because of the pouring rain. Men are embraced fast by the long eyed women because of the shivering cold. The winds moist with rain-water drops, so cool as to remove all the fatigue at the end of competitive amorous sports when the lovers are so fortunate as to be together, even bad raining winter-days become good days.

अर्धं सुप्त्वा निशायाः सरभससुरतायाससन्नश्लथाङ्गः
प्रोद्भूतासह्यतृष्णो मधुमदनिरतो हर्म्यपृष्ठे विविक्ते।
सम्भोगक्लान्तकान्ताशिथिलभुजलतावर्जितं कर्करीतो
ज्योत्स्नाभिन्नाच्छधारं पिबति न सलिलं शारदं मन्दपुण्यः॥९६॥

Having slept half the night, and become tired by keen vigorous amorous sports begun after mid-night with limbs all weary and a burning thirst in an intoxicated state alone with his love in the storied mansion, a lover unless extra-ordinarily unfortunate-drinks the water (boiled and cooled) poured by the tired hand of his beloved equally fatigued.

हेमन्ते दधितुग्धसर्पिरशना माञ्जिष्ठवासोभृतः
काश्मीरद्रवसान्द्रदिग्धवपुषश्छिन्ना विचित्रै रतैः।
वृत्तोरुस्तनकामिनीजनकृताश्लेषा गृहाभ्यन्तरे
ताम्बूलीदलपूगपूरितमुखा धन्याः सुखं शेरते॥९७॥

In the Hemanta season, fortunate men lie happily inside embraced by their loving sweethearts with circular big breasts, with their mouth filled with betal leaf, cuds by them with various amorous sports in intervals, wearing safforn- coloured clothes, their bodies annointed with keśarī paste, after having taken food with curds, milk and ghee.

प्रोद्यत्प्रौढप्रियङ्गुद्युतिभृति विकसत्कुन्दमाद्याद्विरेफे
काले प्रालेयवातप्रचलविलसितोदारमन्दारधाम्नि।
येषां नो कण्ठलग्ना क्षणमपि तुहिनक्षोददक्षा मृगाक्षी
तेषामायामियामा यमसदनसमा यामिनी याति यूनाम्॥९८॥

In the season when the bees are in the height of joy because of 'kunda' flowers resembling *'priyangu'* blooming just then and living in a house with big *'pārijāta'* tree moving by the blowing cold winds, bringing dew drops. If young men have not the furtune to be clung hard by deer-eyed women with their warm breasts dispelling the chill of the dew drops even for a short while, the long night will be like a hell to them.

चुम्बन्तो गण्डभित्तीरलकवति मुखे सीत्कृतान्यादधाना
वक्षस्सूत्कञ्चुकेषु स्तनभरपुलकोद्भेदमापादयन्तः।
ऊरूनाकम्पयन्तः पृथुजघनतटात्स्रंसयन्तोंऽशुकानि
व्यक्तं कान्ताजनानां विटचरितभृतः शैशिरा वान्ति वाताः॥९९॥

The cold winds of the cold season act like cold lovers in regard to women in that they kiss the cheeks producing a long involuntary sound like sin on account of the unbearable chill causing the hairs to stand on end in their bosom and their breasts though covered, causing their thighs to shake in the chillness and making the cloth slip from their big buttocks.

केशानाकुलयन्दृशो मुकुलयन्वासो बलादाक्षिप-
न्नातन्वन्पुलकोद्गमं प्रकटयन्नावेगकम्पं शनैः।
बारंबारमुदारसीत्कृतकुतो दन्तच्छदान्पीडय-
न्प्रायः शैशिर एष सम्प्रति मरुत्कान्तासु कान्तायते॥१००॥

This cold winter wind acts mostly like a lover in regard to women, scattering the hairs of their threads, causing their eye-lids to close, forcibly pulling their clothes, making their hairs stand on end in their body, slowly causing their limbs to shake, blowing over their limbs causing pain, and producing frequently the protesting *sitkāra*-cry.

इति भर्तृहरिविरचितं शृङ्गारशतकं समाप्तम्

३

वैराग्यशतकम्

चूडोत्तंसितचारुचन्द्रकलिकाचञ्चच्छिखाभास्वरो
लीलादग्धविलोलकामशलभः श्रेयोदशाग्रे स्फुरन्।
अन्तःस्फूर्जदपारमोहतिमिरप्राग्भारमुच्छेदयं-
श्चेतःसद्मनि योगिनां विजयते ज्ञानप्रदीपो हरः॥१॥

Hara, the powerful lamp of knowledge, shines bright in the house of the heart of ascetics, the lamp, which is resplendent with the flickering flame of light from the beautiful digit of the moon, worn as crest-ornament, which burnt, with ease, the moth in the shape of bustling Kāma (the god of love), which sheds it quivering light at the top of the wick of supreme happiness and which completely destroys the mass of darkness of unbounded infatuation existing in the heart.

भ्रान्तं देशमनेकदुर्गविषमं प्राप्तं न किञ्चित्फलं
त्यक्त्वा जातिकुलाभिमानमुचितं सेवा कृता निष्फला।
भुक्तं मानविवर्जितं परगृहेष्वाशंकया काकव-
त्तृष्णे जृम्भसि पापकर्मनिरते नाद्यापि सन्तुष्यसि॥२॥

I roamed many inaccessible and perilous places, (but) did not obtain wealth; I served sacrificing proper dignity of caste and family, but all went without any gain; I fed myself being devoid of self-respect like the crows at the house of others in the hope of gain; but oh wretched desire! the instigator of shameless acts! You are not yet satisfied with having humiliated me so mush.

उत्खातं निधिशङ्कया क्षितितलं ध्माता गिरेर्धातवो
निस्तीर्णः सरितां पतिर्नृपतयो यत्नेन संतोषिताः।
मन्त्राराधनतत्परेण मनसा नीताः श्मशाने निशाः
प्राप्तः काणवराटकोऽपि न मया तृष्णेऽधुना मुञ्च माम्॥३॥

I dug up the earth expecting to find a treasure; smelted the ores found in mountains; crossed the ocean, assiduously propitiated kings; passed several nights in the cemetery solely intent upon securing the efficacy of incantations; but I did not obtain even a broken cowrie. Leave me now, then, Oh Greed!

खलोल्लापाः सोढाः कथमपि तदाराधनपरै–
र्निगृह्यान्तर्बाष्पं हसितमपि शून्येन मनसा।
कृतश्चित्तस्तम्भः प्रतिहतधियामञ्जलिरपि
त्वमाशेऽमोघाशे किमपरमतो नर्तयसि माम्॥४॥

Oh Desire! You of ungratified yearning! In our servile attendance on the (wealthy) wicked, their shabby manners and talk we have somehow put up with; suppressing tears that welled up from our hearts, we have smiled out of vacant minds; obeisance we have made to dullards stultified by too much wealth; in what more fooleries would you have me dance.

अमीषां प्राणानां तुलितबिसिनीपत्रपयसां
कृते किं नास्माभिर्विगलितविवेकैर्व्यवसितम्।
यदाढ्यानामग्रे द्रविणमदनिःसंज्ञमनसां
कृतं वीतव्रीडैर्निजगुणकथापातकमपि॥५॥

What have we not endeavoured to do, with our depraved conscience, for the sake of our *Prāṇas* which are unreliable and compared to water on the leaves of a lotus. In presence of the rich, with their minds stupefied by the pride of wealth, we have shamelessly committed the sin of recounting our own merits.

क्षान्तं न क्षमया गृहोचितसुखं त्यक्तं न संतोषतः
सोढा दुःसहशीतवाततपनाः क्लेशान्न तप्तं तपः।
ध्यातं वित्तमहर्निशं नियमितप्राणैर्न शंभोः पदं
तत्तत्कर्म कृतं यदेव मुनिभिस्तैस्तैः फलैर्वञ्चिताः॥६॥

We have forgiven but not out of forgiveness (but out of

our incapacity to correct our wrongs); we have renounced the comforts of home life, but not out of contentment after satisfaction (but as an exile from home in quest of riches) though we have suffered in *clemercies* of weather, cold and heat so difficult to bear, still it is no religious austerities that we have undergone; with subdued vital forces; night and day we have brooded on money, not on the feet of Śiva; thus we have performed those very acts which the saintly recluses do perform, but of their good effect we have deprived ourselves.

भोगा न भुक्ता वयमेव भुक्ता-
स्तपो न तप्तं वयमेव तप्ताः।
कालो न यातो वयमेव याता-
स्तृष्णा न जीर्णा वयमेव जीर्णाः॥७॥

We have not enjoyed pleasures, but we are enjoyed. We have not practised austerities, but we have been harassed (by worldly cares); time has not lapsed but the lease of our life; our greed has not decayed but we have been decayed.

वलिभिर्मुखमाक्रान्तं पलितैरङ्कितं शिरः।
गात्राणि शिथिलायन्ते तृष्णैका तरुणायते॥८॥

Wrinkles have made an inroad on the face; the head is marked with gray hair; all the limbs have become feeble. Greed alone keeps its vigour fresh.

निवृत्ता भोगेच्छा पुरुषबहुमानो विगलितः
समानाः स्वर्याताः सपदि सुहृदो जीवितसमाः।
शनैर्यष्ट्युत्थानं घनतिमिररुद्धे च नयने
अहो धृष्टः कायस्तदपि मरणापायचकितः॥९॥

The desire for enjoyments is lost; the pride of youth is quite; humbled co-eval friends, valued as life itself, have sped quick to heaven; (I have) to stand up slowly supported on a staff; and the eyes are obstructed by powerful blindness; oh the impudence of the body! It is still afraid of being overtaken by death.

आशा नाम नदी मनोरथजला तृष्णातरङ्गाकुला
रागग्राहवती वितर्कविहगा धैर्यद्रुमध्वंसिनी।
मोहावर्तसुदुस्तरातिगहना प्रोत्तुङ्गचिन्तातटी
तस्याः पारगता विशुद्धमनसो नन्दन्ति योगीश्वराः॥१०॥

Desire is, indeed, a river, with the objects of desire for its water, agitated by waves in the form of hankerings, having for sharks the passions, and for birds the misgivings (of the heart), destroying the tree of fortitude, difficult to cross on account of eddies in the form of infatuation, very deep and having anxiety for its sleep banks; the great ascetics of pure heart, who have crossed it, enjoy felicity.

न संसारोत्पन्नं चरितमनुपश्यामि कुशलं
विपाकः पुण्यानां जनयति भयं मे विमृशतः।
महद्भिः पुण्योघैश्चिरपरिगृहीताश्च विषया
महान्तो जायन्ते व्यसनमिव दातुं विषयिणाम्॥११॥

I do not find the virtuous distinction produced by ceremonial observances through life after life to be conducive to well-being, for the sum of such virtuous merits when weighed in mind inspires fear in me. Enjoyments earned by great accession of merit multiply so greatly in the case of people attached to them only to bring them misery and peril.

अवश्यं यातारश्चिरतरमुषित्वापि विषया
वियोगे को भेदस्त्यजति न जनो यत्स्वयममून्।
व्रजन्तः स्वातन्त्र्यादतुलपरितापाय मनसः
स्वयं त्यक्त्वा ह्येते शमसुखमनन्तं विदधति॥१२॥

The objects of pleasure, we dote upon, however they may exist, must of necessity disappear sooner or later. Why should not the pleasure–hunter try to make credit for deliberately abandoning them with scorn and disgust when their loss and the parting from them is absolutely certain. If the objects of pleasure by themselves leave as by casualty or otherwise, their parting causes limitless mortification to the mind, but if we leave them by our own strength of mind and suppression of our desires, the abstention will give us infinite joy in the from of spiritual tranquility.

ब्रह्मज्ञानविवेकनिर्मलधियः कुर्वन्त्यहो दुष्करं
यन्मुञ्चन्त्युपभोगवन्त्यपि धनान्येकान्ततो निःस्पृहाः।
न प्राप्तानि पुरा न संप्रति न च प्राप्तौ दृढप्रत्ययो
वाञ्छामात्रपरिग्रहाण्यपि परं त्यक्तुं न शक्ता वयम्॥१३॥

Oh! It is wonder that men with minds purified by vedāntic discipline and the dawn of Brahmic knowledge achieve the miracle of total abnegation of wealth in their ownership and enjoyment, discarding all desire for them whereas we fail to renounce enjoyments which are reaped by us as mere longings and which we never did realise in the past nor do we realise at present.

धन्यानां गिरिकन्दरे निवसतां ज्योतिः परं ध्यायता-
मानन्दाश्रुजलं पिबन्ति शकुना निःशङ्कमङ्केशयाः।
अस्माकं तु मनोरथोपरचितप्रासादवापीतट-
क्रीडाकाननकेलिकौतुकजुषामायुः परिक्षीयते॥१४॥

Blessed are those who lie in mountain–caves meditating on Brahman, the Supreme light, while birds devoid of fear perch on their laps and drink the tear-drops of bliss while our life is fast ebbing away in the excitement of revelry in palatial mansions or on the banks of refreshing pools or in pleasure-gardens, all created merely by imagination.

भिक्षाशनं तदपि नीरसमेकवारं
शय्या च भूः परिजनो निजदेहमात्रम्।
वस्त्रं च जीर्णशतखण्डमयी च कन्था
हा हा तथापि विषयान्न जहाति चेतः॥१५॥

Alas! The mind does not give up its longing for carnal pleasures even when one has to eat food obtained by begging, and that too unsubstantial and once only in a day; when one has the earth for a couch, and only one's self for an attendant, and when one's raiment is a wallet of a hundred thread bare rags stitched together.

स्तनौ मांसग्रन्थी कनककलशावित्युपमितौ
मुखं श्लेष्मागारं तदपि च शशाङ्केन तुलितम्।
स्रवन्मूत्रक्लिन्नं करिवरशिरःस्पर्धि जघन-
महो निन्द्यं रूपं कविजनविशेषैर्गुरु कृतम्॥१६॥

The breasts which are fleshy protuberances are compared to golden jars; the mouth which is the receptacle of phlegm is likened to the moon; the lips are described as rivalling the head of an elephant king. Mark, how the despicable form (of a woman) has been heightened by a group of poets.

अजानन्माहात्म्यं पततु शलभो दीपदहने
स मीनोऽप्यज्ञानाद्बडिशमुतमश्नातु पिशितम्।
विजानन्तोऽप्येते वयमिह विपज्जालजटिला-
न्न मुञ्चामः कामानह ह गहनो मोहमहिमा॥१७॥

Let an insect fall into flames of the glowing fire without knowing its burning power; let the fish, which does not know the danger, eat the bait attached to the hook. But why should we, having full discernment, not renounce the sensual desires, complicated as they are with manifold dangers? Alas, how inscrutable is the power of delusion?

एको रागिषु राजते प्रियतमादेहार्धहारी हरे।
नीरागेषु जनो विमुक्तललनासङ्गे न यस्मात्परः।
दुर्वारस्मरबाणपन्नगविषव्यासङ्गमुग्धो जनः
शेषः कामविडम्बितान्न विषयान्भोक्तुं न मोक्तुं क्षमः॥१८॥

One Śiva, who is obtained half of his wife's body, shines among the persons who are attached to the objects, only one (Jina or Buddha) shines without being attached to the ladies. All others not being free from the poison of snake in the form of unavaidable arrow of Kāmadeva is neither able to reject the wordly objects nor to enjoy them fully being under the pressure of the desires.

तृषा शुष्यत्यास्ये पिबति सलिलं स्वादु सुरभि
क्षुधार्तः सञ्शालिं कवलयति शाकादिवलितान्।
प्रदीप्ते कामाग्नौ सुदृढतरमाश्लिष्यति वधूं
प्रतीकारं व्याधेः सुखमिति विपर्यस्यति जनः॥१९॥

Man wrongly considers the removal of pain as happiness itself when the mouth is parched with thirst, drinks sweet and fragrant water, when oppressed with hunger, swallows rice mixed with vegetable and other condiments and when the fire of love is kindled he clasps his wife closely.

तुङ्गं वेश्म सुताः सतामभिमताः संख्यातिगाः संपदः
कल्याणी दयिता वयश्च नवमित्यज्ञानमूढो जनः।
मत्वा विश्वमनश्वरं निविशते संसारकारागृहे
संदृश्य क्षणभङ्गुरं तदखिलं धन्यस्तु संन्यस्यति॥२०॥

Possessed of tall mansions, of sons esteemed by the learned, of untold wealth, of a beloved wife full of beneficence, and of youthful age, and thinking this would to be permanent, men deluded by ignorance run into this prison-house of worldiness; whereas blessed indeed is he who considering the transciency of the same world renounces it.

दीना दीनमुखैः सदैव शिशुकैराकृष्टजीर्णाम्बरा
क्रोशद्भिः क्षुधितैर्निरन्नविधुरा दृश्या न चेद्गेहिनी।
याच्ञाभङ्गभयेन गद्गदगलत्त्रुट्यद्विलीनाक्षरं
को 'देहीति' वदेत्स्वदग्धजठरस्यार्थे मनस्वी जनः॥२१॥

If one had no occasion to see one's wife suffering without food and sore aggrieved at the constant sight of hungry crying children with piteous looks pulling at her worn out clothes what self respecting man would for the mere sake of his own petty stomach utter "give me" is a voice faltering and sticking at the throat for fear of his prayer being refused?

अभिमतमहामानग्रन्थिप्रभेदपटीयसी
गुरुतरगुणग्रामाम्भोजस्फुटोज्ज्वलचन्द्रिका।
विपुलविलसल्लज्जावल्लीवितानकुठारिका
जठरपिठरी दुष्पूरेयं करोति विडम्बनाम्॥२२॥

The pit of our stomach so hard to fill is the root indeed of no small undoing : it is ingenious in severing the vital knots, as it were, of our fond self-respect; it is like the bright moonlight shining on the lotus of highly estimable virtues; it is the hatched that hews down the luxuriant creepers of our great modesty.

पुण्ये ग्रामे वने वा महति सितपटच्छन्नपालीं कपाली-
मादाय न्यायगर्भद्विजहुतहुतभुग्धूमधूम्रोपकण्ठम्।
द्वारं द्वारं प्रविष्टो वरमुदरदरीपूरणाय क्षुधार्तो
मानी प्राणी स्वदेशे न पुनरनुदिनं तुल्यकुल्येषु दीनः॥२३॥

A man with self-respect when tortured by hunger would rather, for the sake of filling the cavity of the stomach, wander about a large forest, or with a broken pot whose edge is covered with a white piece of cloth, goes about in a holy city from door to door the sills of which have been darkened by smoke arising from the fire into which oblations have been thrown by Brahmins versed in the rituals, but will never be a constant suppliant among his equals in his own country.

गङ्गातरङ्गहिमशीकरशीतलानि
विद्याधराध्युषितचारुशिलातलानि।
स्थानानि किं हिमवतः प्रलयं गतानि
यत्सावमानपरपिण्डरता मनुष्याः॥२४॥

Why should men run eagerly after doles of food to other peoples' door, exposing themselves to disgrace? Have the holy and lovely Himālaya retreats, moist with drops of Gaṅgā waves and habited by celestial Vidyādharas, been destroyed by cataclysm?

किं कन्दाः कन्दरेभ्यः प्रलयमुपगता निर्झरा वा गिरिभ्यः
प्रध्वस्ता वा तरुभ्यः सरसफलभृतो वल्कलिन्यश्च शाखाः।
वीक्ष्यन्ते यन्मुखानि प्रसभमुपगतप्रश्रयाणां खलानां
दुःखोपात्ताल्पवित्तस्मयपवनवशानर्तितभ्रूलतानि॥२५॥

Or is it that the herbs and roots have all disappeared from caves, and streams from hillsides, or branches of trees bearing luscious fruits and yielding barks are all destroyed, the faces of wretches, perfectly devoid of good breeding, are found to have their eye-brows dancing like creepers in the wind of an arrogance which their scanty earning eked out with hardship engenders in them?

पुण्यैर्मूलफलैः प्रियैश्च सलिलैर्वृत्तिं कुरुष्वाधुना
भूशय्यां नववल्कलैरकरुणैरुत्तिष्ठ यामो वनम्।
क्षुद्राणामविवेकमूढमनसां यत्रेश्वराणां सदा
वित्तव्याधिविकारविह्वलगिरां नामापि न श्रूयते॥२६॥

Get up, let us go to the forest where even the name is not heard of the narrow hearted rich persons whose minds are blunt through coarseness and whose speech is agitated by the effects of the malady of lucre. There in the forest maintain yourself now on pure roots and fruits and agreeable water, making the earth your bed, and the rough barks of trees your new coverlet.

फलं स्वेच्छालभ्यं प्रतिवनमखेदं क्षितिरुहां
पयः स्थाने स्थाने शिशिरमधुरं पुण्यसरिताम्।
मुदुस्पर्शा शय्या सुललितलतापल्लवमयी
सहन्ते संतापं तदपि धनिनां द्वारि कृपणाः॥२७॥

There are the fruits of trees obtainable at will in every forest without difficulty; at intervals there is the cool and sweet water of sacred rivers; a bed made up of the tender leaves of creepers is soft to touch; mean persons do yet suffer from pain at the gates of the rich.

ये वर्धन्ते धनपतिपुरःप्रार्थनादुःखभाजो
ये चाल्पत्वं दधति विषयाक्षेपपर्यस्तबुद्धेः।
तेषामन्तःस्फुरितहसितं वासराणां स्मरेयं
ध्यानच्छेदे शिखरिकुहरग्रावशय्यानिषण्णः॥२८॥

Seated on a stony couch in the cavern of a mountain, may I, in the intervals of contemplation, recall, with an inward *smile,* those days, which seem to be longer to one experiencing the misery of (having to address) supplications to the wealthy and which (days) appear to be shorter (to one) whose mind is tossed about by the allurement of sensual objects.

ये संतोषसुखप्रबुद्धमनसस्तेषां न भिन्ना मुदो
ये त्वन्ये धनलोभसंकुलधियस्तेषां न तृष्णा हता।
इत्थं कस्य कृते कृतः स विधिना तादृक्पदं संपदां
स्वात्मन्येव समाप्तहेममहिमा मेरुर्न मे रोचते॥२९॥

The pleasures of those who are constantly satisfied with contentment are never altered, while the desire of those, whose minds are engrossed with lust after riches, never ceases, then for whose sake was Meru so full of wealth, created by the creator? Its golden splendour is confined to itself alone. I don't like it.

भिक्षाहारमदैन्यमप्रतिसुखं भीतिच्छिदं सर्वदा
दुर्मात्सर्यमदाभिमानमथनं दुःखौघविध्वंसनम्।
सर्वत्रान्वहमप्रयत्नसुलभं साधुप्रियं पावनं
शम्भोः सत्रमवार्यमक्षयनिधिं शंसन्ति योगीश्वराः॥३०॥

The great ascetics say that the great cult of Śiva is a treasure of inexhaustible happiness which cannot be refused to any one– a cult in which there is maintenance on charity, in which there is no degradation, which yields unparrelled happiness, which always remove fear, does away with the haughty pride resulting from the wicked jealously, and counteracts the current of miseries which is easily excessible every day at all places, is preferred by the good and is holy.

भोगे रोगभयं कुले च्युतिभयं वित्ते नृपालाद्भयं
मानेे दैन्यभयं बले रिपुभयं रूपे जराया भयम्।
शास्त्रे वादिभयं गुणे खलभयं काये कृतान्ताद्भयं
सर्वं वस्तु भयान्वितं भुवि नृणां वैराग्यमेवाभयम्॥३१॥

Enjoyment is accompained with the fear of disease, noble birth is liable to fall, wealth is exposed to danger from the king, dignity to misfortune, an army to fear from the enemy, beauty to danger from old age, knowledge of Śāstras to controversy, merits to danger from the wicked and body to the fear of death. All objects are thus beset with danger; asceticism alone is invulnerable on earth.

आक्रान्तं मरणेन जन्म जरसा विद्युच्चलं यौवनं
संतोषो धनलिप्सया शमसुखं प्रौढाङ्गनाविभ्रमैः।
लोकैर्मत्सरिभिर्गुणा वनभुवो व्यालैर्नृपा दुर्जनै-
रस्थैर्येण विभूतयोऽप्युपहता ग्रस्तं न किं केन वा॥३२॥

Birth is attended with death; vivacious youth with old age; contentment with cupidity; the felicity of renunciation stands in the danger of being disturted by the sportive movements of youthful women, and virtues by malicious people; wood-lands are infested by serpents; kings are surrounded by wicked people; even prosperity is effected by inconstancy; or what is there that is not usurped by something else?

आधिव्याधिशतैर्जनस्य विविधैरारोग्यमुन्मूल्यते
लक्ष्मीर्यत्र पतन्ति तत्र विवृतद्वारा इव व्यापदः।
जातं जातमवश्यमाशु विवशं मृत्युः करोत्यात्मसा-
त्तत्किं नाम निरङ्कुशेन विधिना यन्निर्मितं सुस्थिरम्॥३३॥

The health of man is undermined by hundreds of mental and physical infirmities; to that place where wealth exists, misfortunes come thronging as if through gates thrown open to them, death hastily asserts his supremacy over every helpless creature that is born; what thing is there then, that despotic fate has made immune from danger?

भोगास्तुङ्गतरङ्गभङ्गचपलाः प्राणाः क्षणध्वंसिनः
स्तोकान्येव दिनानि यौवनसुखं प्रीतिः प्रियष्वस्थिरा।
तत्संसारमसारमेव निखिलं बुध्वा बुधा बोधका
लोकानुग्रहपेशलेन मनसा यत्नः समाधीयताम्।।३४।।

Enjoyments are transient like high surging waves; life is liable to pass away in a moment; youthful happiness lasts for a few days only; love for the cherished is fickle; knowing therefore that the entire worldly existence is destitute of any good, wise men, givers of advice, make attempts with a mind skillful in doing good to the people.

भोगा मेघवितानमध्यविलसत्सौदामिनीचञ्चला
आयुर्वायुविघट्टिताभ्रपटलीलीनाम्बुवद्भङ्गुरम्।।
लोला यौवनलालसास्तनुभृतामित्याकलय्य द्रुतं
योगे धैर्यसमाधिसिद्धिसुलभे बुद्धिं विधध्वं बुधाः।।३५।।

The pleasures of the world are fleeting like the lightning in the conopy of the sky covered by clouds. Life is short-lived like water-drops sticking in the lotus-leaf tossed with the winds. The desires for pleasures, common in youth may fade and die later on. Wise men! Reflect upon all these and quickly turn your minds towards the practice of yoga which could easily be achieved by persevering and firm concentration and *samādhi*–union with beloved object of meditation.

आयुः कल्लोललोलं कतिपयदिवसस्थायिनी यौवनश्री-
रर्थाः संकल्पकल्पा घनसमयतडिद्विभ्रमा भोगपूराः।
कण्ठाश्लेषोपगूढं तदपि च न चिरं यत्प्रियाभिः प्रणीतं
ब्रह्मण्यासक्तचित्ता भवत भवभयाम्भोधिपारं तरीतुम्।।३६।।

Life is fickle like a swelling wave; the splendour of youth remains only for some days, wealth is momentary like thought; pleasures are like the flashes of lightning in autumn; even the embrace of the beloved, encircling the neck, lasts not for a long time; so have your attention concentrated upon Brahman to cross the ocean of the terrible fear of birth in the world.

कृच्छ्रेणामेध्यमध्ये नियमिततनुभिः स्थीयते गर्भवासे
कान्ताविश्लेषदुःखव्यतिकरविषमो यौवने विप्रयोगः।
नारीणामप्यवज्ञा विलसति नियतं वृद्धभावोऽप्यसाधुः
संसारे रे मनुष्या वदत यदि सुखं स्वल्पमप्यस्ति किंचित्॥३७॥

With their bodies cramped, men have to remain with difficulty in the womb in the midst of impurities; in youth the enjoyments of pleasures is difficult on account of the distraction arising from the pain of separation from one's beloved; surely old age too is unwelcome, the refractoriness of women is conspicuous; say oh men, if there is even the least happiness in worldly life.

व्याघ्रीव तिष्ठति जरा परितर्जयन्ती
रोगाश्च शत्रव इव प्रहरन्ति देहम्।
आयुः परिस्त्रवति भिन्नघटादिवाम्भो
लोकस्तथाप्यहितमाचरतीति चित्रम्॥३८॥

Old age looms frightening men like a tigress; diseases afflict the body like enemies; life is flowing away like water running out of a leaky vessel; still, how wonderful is that man goes on doing wicked deeds.

भोगा भङ्गुरवृत्तयो बहुविधास्तैरेव चायं भव-
स्तत्कस्येह कृते परिभ्रमत रे लोकाः कृतं चेष्टितैः।
आशापाशशतोपशान्तिविशदं चेतः समाधीयतां
कामोत्पत्तिवशे स्वधामनि यदि श्रद्धेयमस्मद्वचः॥३९॥

The enjoyments are multifarious and of a transient nature; and by them is constituted this worldy life; what for should you then wander; oh people! Refrain from your actions. If our word is to be believed, concentrate your mind, pure on account of the snapping of the bonds of desires, within its cell which can be within reach when passion is rooted out.

ब्रह्मेन्द्रादिमरुद्गणांस्तृणकणान्यत्र स्थितो मन्यते
यत्स्वादाद्विरसा भवन्ति विभवास्त्रैलोक्यराज्यादयः।
भोगः कोऽपि स एक एव परमो नित्योदितो जृम्भते
भो साधो क्षणभङ्गुरे तदितरे भोगे रतिं मा कृथाः॥४०॥

That indescribable pleasure alone is the highest and ever abiding being in the enjoyment of which one considers the hosts of gods such as Brahmā, Indra and others as straw and after tasting which high states such as the sovereignty of the three worlds and lose all charm. O good man! Do not fix, therefore, your affection on any other enjoyment which is evanescent.

रम्या सा नगरी महान्स नृपतिः सामन्तचक्रं च त-
त्पार्श्वे तस्य च सा विदग्धपरिषत्ताश्चन्द्रबिम्बाननाः।
उद्वृत्तः स च राजपुत्रनिवहस्ते बन्दिनस्ताः कथाः
सर्वं यस्य वशादगात्स्मृतिपथं कालाय तस्मै नमः॥४१॥

That delightful city, that great king, and the circle of feudatory kings, and that assembly with eminent scholars at his side, the ladies with their faces like the disc of the moon, that group of haughty princes, those bards, and those stories now to death through whose (destructive) power, all these things have become the things of past.

यत्रानेके क्वचिदपि गृहे तत्र तिष्ठत्यथैको
यत्राप्येकस्तदनु बहवस्तत्र नैकोऽपि चान्ते।
इत्थं चेमौ रजनिदिवसौ दोलयन्द्वाविवाक्षौ
कालः कल्यो भुवनफलके क्रीडति प्राणिशारैः॥४२॥

Where in some house (or, a square in the case of a chess board) there were many, now there is one, and where there were many successively, there is none at the end. In this manner, the great lord of time dexterous in playing this game sits day and night moving, on the chess board of the world, human beings are like wooden pieces in a sporting spirit.

आदित्यस्य गतागतैरहरहः संक्षीयते जीवितं
व्यापारैर्बहुकार्यभारगुरुभिः कालो न विज्ञायते।
दृष्ट्वा जन्मजराविपत्तिमरणं त्रासश्च नोत्पद्यते
पीत्वा मोहमयीं प्रमादमदिरामुन्मत्तभूतं जगत्॥४३॥

Daily, with the rising and setting of the sun, life shortens, time is not felt on account of affairs heavily burdened with manifold activities. Neither is fear produced at beholding birth, death, old age and suffering. Alas, the world has become mad by drinking the stupefying wine of delusion.

रात्रिः सैव पुनः स एव दिवसो मत्वा मुधा जन्तवो
धावन्त्युद्यमिनस्तथैव निभृतप्रारब्धतत्तत्क्रियाः।
व्यापारैः पुनरुक्तभूतविषयैरेवंविधेनामुना
संसारेण कदर्थिताः कथमहो मोहान्न लज्जामहे॥४४॥

Believing that the night is the same and day is the same, ignorant people run busily in the same manner setting about their diverse vocation. Oh, how do we not, through infatuation, feel ashamed disgraced by transactions in which there is a repetition of the enjoyment of pleasures and by this worldly life of such nature!

न ध्यातं पदमीश्वरस्य विधिवत्संसारविच्छित्तये
स्वर्गद्वारकपाटपाटनपटुर्धर्मोऽपि नोपार्जितः।
नारीपीनपयोधरोरुयुगलं स्वप्नेऽपि नालिङ्गितं
मातुः केवलमेव यौवनवनच्छेदे कुठारा वयम्॥४५॥

We have not contemplated on the feet of the Lord as per the rules for the annihilation of worldly existence; nor did we accumulate religious merit which is capable of throwing open the doors of heaven; nor did wc embrace the pair of the stout breasts and thighs of a beautiful woman even in a dream. We have been axes only in cutting down the youth-forest of our mothers.

नाभ्यस्ता भुवि वादिवृन्ददमनी विद्या विनीतोचिता
खड्गाग्रैः करिकुम्भपीठदलनैर्नाकं न नीतं यशः।।
कान्ताकोमलपल्लवाधररसः पीतो न चन्द्रोदये
तारुण्यं गतमेव निष्फलमहो शून्यालये दीपवत्।।४६।।

We have not acquired knowledge befitting the well-conducted and capable of silencing hosts of disputants in this world; fame has not been exalted to heaven by shattering the vast temples of elephants by the point of the sword, we did not drink of sprout soft lip of our beloved at the rising of the moon. Alas! Our youth has passed off fruitlessly like a lamp buring in an empty house.

विद्या नाधिगता कलङ्करहिता वित्तं च नोपार्जितं
शुश्रूषापि समाहितेन मनसा पित्रोर्न संपादिता।
आलोलायतलोचना युवतयः स्वप्नेऽपि नालिङ्गिताः
कालोऽयं परपिण्डलोलुपतया काकैरिव प्रेर्यते।।४७।।

No learning was acquired with purity. No wealth was acquired, no reverential service was rendered to the parents with compossed and dutiful mind. Women with long eyes were not embraced even in dreams. Time has been spent like crows seeking doles of food and crumbs thrown by others.

वयं येभ्यो जाताश्चिरमपगता एव खलु ते
समं यैः संवृद्धाः स्मृतिविषयतां तेऽपि गमिताः।
इदानीमेते स्मः प्रतिदिवसमासन्नपतना
गतास्तुल्यावस्थां सिकतिलनदीतीरतरुभिः।।४८।।

Those from whom we were born have passed away; those too, with whom we grew up, have been consigned to the region of memory; now we have reduced to the same state as that of trees growing on the bank of a sandy river with the fall approaching nearer and nearer day by day.

आयुर्वर्षशतं नृणां परिमितं रात्रौ तदर्धं गतं
तस्यार्धस्य परस्य चार्धमपरं बालत्ववृद्धत्वयोः।
शेषं व्याधिवियोगदुःखसहितं सेवादिभिर्नीयते
जीवे वारितरङ्गचञ्चलतरे सौख्यं कुतः प्राणिनाम्।।४९।।

The life of a man is limited to one hundred years; half of

it passes in night; of the remaining half, one-half made up of its first and last one-fourths, is occupied by youth and old age. The remainder is passed in servitude etc., accompanied by disease and grief for the separation. Where is there any happiness for mortals in worldly life which is even more unsteady than a wave?

क्षणं बालो भूत्वा क्षणमपि युवा कामरसिकः
क्षणं वित्तैर्हीनः क्षणमपि च संपूर्णविभवः।
जराजीर्णैरङ्गैर्नट इव वलीमण्डिततनु-
र्नरः संसारान्ते विशति यमधानीयवनिकाम्॥५०॥

A man becomes child for a moment and a youth, a destitute for a while and in abundance, like an actor, man makes at the end of his role; when diseased in all limbs by age and wrinkled all over the body, his exit behind the scene that veils the abode of Yama (death).

त्वं राजा वयमप्युपासितगुरुप्रज्ञाभिमानोन्नताः
ख्यातस्त्वं विभवैर्यशांसि कवयो दिक्षु प्रतन्वन्ति नः।
इत्थं मानधनातिदूरमुभयोरप्यावयोरन्तरं
यद्यस्मासु पराङ्मुखोऽसि वयमप्येकान्ततो निस्पृहाः॥५१॥

You are a king. We have reached a great height by the grace of our preceptor of high wisdom and learning at whose feet we sat long with reverence and admiration. You are renowned by your rich possessions and your regal splendours. But poets and men of letters sing far and wide our praise. In this way the gulf between you, and us, of the wealth, of reputation for holiness, is very wide. If you do not turn your back upon us, we, totally desireless as we are, look to you for nothing and do not care for you.

अर्थानामीशिषे त्वं वयमपि च गिरामीश्महे यावदर्थं
शूरस्त्वं वादिदर्पज्वरशमनविधावक्षयं पाटवं नः।
सेवन्ते त्वां धनाढ्या मतिमलहतये मामपि श्रोतुकामा
मय्यप्यास्था न ते चेत्त्वयि मम सुतरामेन राजन्गतोऽस्मि॥५२॥

You are the lord of riches in full, we are too of words in

all their senses; you are brave, our skill in the act of subduing the feverish pride of a controversialist is inexhaustible; those who are filled with wealth serve you; even me serve those who have a longing to listen to me that the taint of their hearts maybe removed; if you have no respect for me, the less have I for you; O king, here am I off.

वयमिह परितुष्टा वल्कलैस्त्वं दुकूलैः
सम इह परितोषो निर्विशेषो विशेषः।
स तु भवति दरिद्रो यस्य तृष्णा विशाला
मनसि च परितुष्टे कोऽर्थवान्को दरिद्रः॥५३॥

We are satisfied with the barks and you are with rich garments; but equal is our contentment, the distinction makes no difference. Poor indeed is he whose desires are boundless. If the mind be contented, who is rich and who is poor?

फलमलमशनाय स्वादु पानाय तोयं
शयनमवनिपृष्ठे वल्कले वाससी च।
नवधनमधुपानभ्रान्तसर्वेन्द्रियाणा-
मविनयमनुमन्तुं नोत्सहे दुर्जनानाम्॥५४॥

Fruits for food, tasteful water for drink, the bare ground for sleep, the barks of trees for cloth are enough. But I do not like approve misbehaviour of evil men whose all senses are led astray by drinking the wine of newly acquired wealth.

अशीमहि वयं भिक्षामाशावासो वसीमहि।
शयीमहि महीपृष्ठे कुर्वीमहि किमीश्वरैः॥५५॥

We live on alms, cover ourselves with the direction garments and sleep on the surface of earth. What will we do with the kings?

न नटा न विटा न गायका
न परद्रोहनिबद्धबुद्धयः।
नृपसद्मनि नाम के वयं
कुचभारानमिता न योषितः॥५६॥

We are neither actors, nor flatterers, nor singers nor the

persons whose intellect is set on others; nor are we women bent down with the burden of the breasts. What will we do in royal palace?

विपुलहृदयैर्धन्यैः कैश्चिज्जगज्जनितं पुरा
विधृतमपरैर्दत्तं चान्यैर्विजित्य तृणं यथा।
इह हि भुवनान्यन्ये धीराश्चतुर्दश भुञ्जते
कतिपयपुरस्वाम्ये पुंसां क एष मदज्वरः॥५७॥

In ancient time this world was created by some largehearted monarches; it was sustained by some and it was conquered and given away like straw by others. Even now, some heroes enjoy the fourteen divisions of this world. For what then this feverish pride of men having achieved sovereignty over a few towns only?

अभुक्तायां यस्यां क्षणमपि न यातं नृपशतै-
र्भुवस्तस्या लाभे क इव बहुमानः क्षितिभुजाम्।
तदंशस्याप्यंशे तदवयवलेशेऽपि पतयो
विषादे कर्तव्ये विदधति जडाः प्रत्युत मुदम्॥५८॥

What high dignity, alas, is there for kings in gaining that earth which has never even for a moment been left unenjoyed by hundreds of rulers! The stupid owners of a shared of the limb of a fraction of its fraction feel delighted, but they ought to grieve.

मृत्पिण्डो जलरेखया बलयितः सर्वोऽप्ययं नन्वणुः
भागीकृत्य तमेव संयुगशतै राज्ञां गणा भुञ्जते।
ते दद्युर्ददतोऽथवा न किमपि क्षुद्रा दरिद्रा भृशं
धिग्धिक्तान्पुरुषाधमान्धनकणान्वाञ्छन्ति तेभ्योऽपि ये॥५९॥

Earth is but a lump of clay circled by a ring of water. Even the whole of it is just a particle. Hosts of kings, having partitioned it after fighting hundreds of battles, enjoy it. These very poor insignificant persons cannot give anything. Nothing is strange for them but downright shame on those mean fellows who would beg bits of coin from them even!

स जातः कोप्यासीन्मदनरिपुणा मूर्ध्नि धवलं
कपालं यस्योच्चैर्विनिहितमलंकारविधये।
नृभिः प्राणत्राणप्रवणमतिभिः कैश्चिदधुना
नमद्भिः कः पुंसामयमतुलदर्पज्वरभरः॥६०॥

He alone is born whose white skull was, by the enemy as the God of love, held prominetly on his head as an ornament; (and yet) what height of morbid presumption is there on the part of men when a few persons solicitous of saving their own lives to them.

परेषां चेतांसि प्रतिदिवसमाराध्य बहुधा
प्रसादं किं नेतुं विशसि हृदय क्लेशकलिलम्।
प्रसन्ने त्वय्येव स्वयमुदितचिन्तामणिगुणे
विमुक्तः संकल्पः किमभिलषितं पुष्यति न ते॥६१॥

Oh heart! Why do you set youself on winning good graces, so hard to secure, by daily propitiating the minds of men in various ways? If you only make your own soul pure making it free from morbid desires, would not the mere wish of that pure *'Ātman'* which has the inherent greatness of a number of '*Cintāmaṇis*' reputed as givers of all that is desired, secure to you immediately the thing you want?

परिभ्रमसि किं मुधा क्वचन चित्त विश्राम्यतां
स्वयं भवति यद्यथा भवति तत्तथा नान्यथा।
अतीतमपि न स्मरन्नपि च भाव्यसंकल्पय-
न्नतर्कितगमागमाननुभवस्व भोगानिह॥६२॥

Why do you wander for nothing? Oh mind! Rest youself somewhere. A thing that naturally takes a particular course does take it; it does not change. Without, therefore, remembering what is past, or speculating about future you experience fruits, the coming and going of which cannot be determined beforehand in this world.

एतस्माद्विरमेन्द्रियार्थगहनादायासकादाश्रय
श्रेयोमार्गमशेषदुःखशमनव्यापारदक्षं क्षणात्।
शान्तं भावमुपैहि संत्यज निजां कल्लोललोलां गतिं
मा भूयो भज भङ्गुरां भवरतिं चेतः प्रसीदाधुना॥६३॥

Oh heart! Be pleased now; do not again run after perishable worldly happiness, cease from entering this troublesome mazy forest in the shape of material objects; take up the way to final absolution, give up your course which is as unsteady as the waves and adopt a peaceful attitude which is capable of putting down all miseries in a moment.

मोहं मार्जय तामुपार्जय रतिं चन्द्रार्धचूडामणौ
चेतः स्वर्गतरङ्गिणीतटभुवामासङ्गमङ्गीकुरु।
को वा वीचिषु बुद्बुदेषु च तडिल्लेखासु च स्त्रीषु च
ज्वालाग्रेषु च पन्नगेषु च सरिद्वेगेषु च प्रत्ययः॥६४॥

Oh my mind! Shake off delusion and be devoted to him who bears the crescent of the moon as an ornament on the head (Śiva); and domicile yourself on the banks of the celestial river. For, what reliance can be placed in waves and bubbles, in streaks of lightening and women, or in the tips of flames, or serpents, or the currents of streams?

चेतश्चिन्तय मा रमां सकृदिमामस्थायिनीमास्थया
भूपालभ्रुकुटीकुटीविहरणव्यापारपण्याङ्गनाम्।
कन्थाकञ्चकिताः प्रविश्य भवनद्वाराणि वाराणसी-
रथ्यापङ्क्तिषु पाणिपात्रपतितां भिक्षामपेक्षामहे॥६५॥

Do not even for a moment, O mind! think fervidly of this unstable goddess of wealth who is like a harlot sporting in the house like eyebrows of kings; entering through the gates of houses in Benares, clad in a wallet, we await in the line of its streets for alms dropped into the palm of our hand serving us as a pot.

अग्रे गीतं सरसकवयः पार्श्वतो दाक्षिणात्याः
पृष्ठे लीलावलयरणितं चामरग्राहिणीनाम्।
यद्यस्त्येवं कुरु भवरसास्वादने लम्पटत्वं
नो चेच्चेतः प्रविश सहसा निर्विकल्पे समाधौ॥६६॥

Oh mind! Be engrossed in the enjoyment of worldly pleasures, if you have songs in front of you, sweet poets from the Deccan by your side and the tinkling of deftly moving bracelets of damsels holding the chawris behind you, otherwise plunge yourself at once into devout concentration freeing you from all consciousness.

प्राप्ताः श्रियः सकलकामदुघास्ततः किं
दत्तं पदं शिरसि विद्विषतां ततः किम्।
संमानिताः प्रणयिनो विभवैस्ततः किं
कल्पं स्थितं तनुभृतां तनुभिस्ततः किम्॥६७॥

What is there, if wealth capable of granting all desires is obtained? What is there, if the foot is placed on the heads of the enemies? What is there, if we honour friends with riches? What is there, if the bodies of mortals have lasted for a *kalpa.*

भक्तिर्भवे मरणजन्मभयं हृदिस्थं
स्नेहो न बन्धुषु न मन्मथजा विकाराः।
संसर्गदोषरहिता विजना वनान्ता
वैराग्यमस्ति किमतः परमर्थनीयम्॥६८॥

If there is devotion to Śiva and the fear of death and birth present to the mind, if there is no attachment to relatives and no mental perturbations caused by the God of Love, if there is a forest uninhabited and free from the fault of contact, and indifference towards worldly life, what else is to be desired?

तस्मादनन्तमजरं परमं विकासि
तद्ब्रह्म चिन्तय किमेभिरसद्विकल्पैः।
यस्यानुषङ्गिण इमे भुवनाधिपत्य-
भोगादयः कृपणलोकमता भवन्ति॥६९॥

Contemplate that Brahman which is endless, undecaying,

sublime and pervading; what is the use of these wrong notions? Sovereignty and other pleasures, approved of by mean people, follow in the train of Brahman.

पातालमाविशसि यासि नभो विलङ्घ्य
दिङ्मण्डलं भ्रमसि मानस चापलेन।
भ्रान्त्यापि जातु विमलं कथमात्मलीनं
तद् ब्रह्म न स्मरसि निर्वृतिमेषि येन॥७०॥

Being thus agitated, oh mind! thou descend into the nether regions, roar up beyond the skies, and wander all around the four quarters. Why, even by mistake, you do not concentrate on that Brahman, of the nature of self and bereft of all imperfections, whereby you may attain supreme bliss!

किं वेदैः स्मृतिभिः पुराणपठनैः शास्त्रैर्महाविस्तरैः
स्वर्गग्रामकुटीनिवासफलदैः कर्मक्रियाविभ्रमैः।
मुक्त्वैकं भवबन्धदुःखरचनाविध्वंसकालानलं
स्वात्मानन्दपदप्रवेशकलनं शेषा वणिग्वृत्तयः॥७१॥

What is there in Vedas, Smṛtis, in the readings of mythology, the vast Śāstras, or the mazes of ceremonials, which give us, as their fruits, a resting-place in heaven, (which is, as it were) a village interspersed with huts! All else is but the bargaining of traders except that one way which admits one into the state of supreme bliss in one's self, and which is like the final destructive fire to consume the evolving mass of worldly miseries.

यदा मेरुः श्रीमान्निपतति युगान्ताग्निनिहतः
समुद्राः शुष्यन्ति प्रचुरनिकरग्राहनिलयाः।
धरा गच्छत्यन्तं धरणिधरपादैरपि धृता
शरीरे का वार्ता करिकलभकर्णाग्रचपले॥७२॥

When the great mountain Meru struck by the fire at the time of the destruction of world falls; when the seas which are the abode of a large number of sharks get dry up; when the earth supported by the feet of mount, why talk of a human body which is unsteady like the end of a young elephant's ear?

गात्रं संकुचितं गतिर्विगलिता भ्रष्टा च दन्तावलि-
दृष्टिर्नश्यति वर्धते बधिरता वक्त्रं च लालायते।
वाक्यं नाद्रियते च बान्धवजनो भार्या न शुश्रूषते
हा कष्टं पुरुषस्य जीर्णवयसः पुत्रोऽप्यमित्रायते॥७३॥

In old age the body is shrivelled, the gait falters, the row of teeth is displaced, the vision is obscured, deafness grows, and mouth slobbers; the relatives do not obey the orders and wife does not serve; alas! even the son acts inimically towards an aged man.

वर्णं सितं शिरसि वीक्ष्य शिरोरुहाणां
स्थानं जरापरिभवस्य यदेव पुंसाम्।
आरोपितास्थिशकलं परिहृत्य यान्ति
चण्डालकूपमिव दूरतरं तरुण्यः॥७४॥

Seeing the white colour of the hair on the head when men are defeated by old age, young ladies go away leaving them at a distance, as they leave a well used by low-castes over which a piece of bone is suspended.

यावत्स्वस्थमिदं शरीरमरुजं यावज्जरा दूरतो
यावच्चेन्द्रियशक्तिरप्रतिहता यावत्क्षयो नायुषः।
आत्मश्रेयसि तावदेव विदुषा कार्यः प्रयत्नो महा-
न्संदीप्ते भवने तु कूपखननं प्रत्युद्यमः कीदृशः॥७५॥

As long as this body is free from disease and decrepitude, as long as senility is far off, as long as the powers of the senses are unaffected and life is not decaying, so long, wise persons should put forth mighty exertions for the sake of their supreme good, for when the house is on fire what setting about digging a well?

तपस्यन्तः सन्तः किमधिनिवसामः सुरनदीं
गुणोदारान्दारानुत परिचरामः सविनयम्।
पिबामः शास्त्रौघानुत विविधकाव्यामृतरसा-
न्न विद्मः किं कुर्मः कतिपयनिमेषायुषि जने॥७६॥

Shall we go and live on the bank of the holy Gaṅgā and

perform *Tapas* there? a shall we amiably serve (our) wives graced by virtues; shall we drink the currents of scriptural literature, or of the nectar of diverse poetical literature? We do not know what to do within this life which is limited to a short time.

दुराराध्याश्चामी तुरगचलचित्ताः क्षितिभुजो
वयं तु स्थूलेच्छा महति च पदे बद्धमनसः।
जरा देहं मृत्युर्हरति सकलं जीवितमिदं
सखे नान्यच्छ्रेयो जगति विदुषोऽन्यत्र तपसः॥७७॥

These kings are difficult to please with their unsteady minds galloping like unruly horses. But we are entertaining hopes of getting rich presents of money from them. Old age is taking away all strength and alertness from the body. Death is waiting to take away our dear life. Friend! There is nothing better for the wise man than *tapas*.

माने म्लायिनि खण्डिते च वसुनि व्यर्थे प्रयातेऽर्थिनि
क्षीणे बन्धुजने गते परिजने नष्टे शनैर्यौवने।
युक्तं केवलमेतदेव सुधियां यज्जह्नुकन्यापयः-
पूतग्रावगिरीन्द्रकन्दरदरीकुञ्जे निवासः क्वचित्॥७८॥

Pride being on the decline, fortune being, the mendicant having gone without gaining relations having diminished in number, attendants having gone away, and youth having gradually died out, only one thing is proper for the wise viz. a habitation somewhere in a brake in a cavern of the mountain, the rocks of which are purified by the waters of the Gaṅgā.

रम्याश्चन्द्रमरीचयस्तृणवती रम्या वनान्तस्थली
रम्यं साधुसुहृत्समागमसुखं काव्येषु रम्याः कथाः।
कोपोपाहितवाष्पबिन्दुतरलं रम्यं प्रियाया मुखं
सर्वं रम्यमनित्यतामुपगते चित्ते न किंचित्पुनः॥७९॥

Delightful are the moon-beams, delightful is the forest spot verdant with grass, the happiness arising from the company of the good people and friends is gratifying; the narratives in poetic works are pleasing; charming is the face of the beloved shining with the tears deposited on it by anger; everything is charming but nothing is charming when the mind is destracted.

रम्यं हर्म्यतलं न किं वसतये श्राव्यं न गेयादिकं
किं वा प्राणसमासमागमसुखं नैवाधिकं प्रीतये।
किं तु भ्रान्तपतङ्गपक्षपवनव्यालोलदीपाङ्कुर-
च्छायाचञ्चलमाकलय्य सकलं सन्तो वनान्तं गताः॥८०॥

Is there not a delightful mansion for habitation; is not music etc. pleasing to the ear; is not the happiness of the company of one as dear as life itself to a man's great gratification? But wise men have resorted to the forest considering all this as unstable as the shadow of a small lamp flickering in the wind of a moth's wing madly falling upon it.

आसंसारं त्रिभुवनमिदं चिन्वतां तात ताह-
नवास्माकं नयनपदवीं श्रोत्रमार्गं गतो वा।
योऽयं धत्ते विषयकरिणीगाढगूढाभिमान-
क्षीबस्यान्तःकरणकरिणः संयमालानलीलाम्॥८१॥

O friend! While searching this triple world as far as worldly life prevails, none has come within the range of our sight or hearing as can easily become the post for fastening, by means of self-restraint, the elephant of the mind intoxicated by the deep-seated and secret attachment for the female elephant in the form of the sensual objects.

यदेतत्स्वच्छन्दं विहरणमकार्पण्यमशनं
सहार्यैः संवासः श्रुतमुपशमैकव्रतफलम्।
मनो मन्दस्पन्दं बहिरपि चिरस्यापि विमृश-
न्न जाने कस्यैषा परिणतिरुदारस्य तपसः॥८२॥

Though reflecting for a long time, I do not know of what great penance this is the result. *viz.* this rambling at will, this meal free from humiliation, the company of the noble, this learning having for its fruits the observance of the one vow of controlling the senses, and the mind moving slowely towards external objects.

जीर्णा एव मनोरथाः स्वहृदये यातं च तद्यौवनं
हन्ताङ्गेषु गुणाश्च वन्ध्यफलतां याता गुणज्ञैर्विना।
किं युक्तं सहसाभ्युपैति बलवान्कालः कृतान्तोऽक्षमी
ह्यज्ञातं स्मरशासनाङ्घ्रियुगलं मुक्त्वास्ति नान्या गतिः॥८३॥

Desires have already been absorbed in the heart; youth has passed away; and alas! in the absence of appreciaters of merit, skill in the limbs has proved fruitless; relentless and powerful death, the all-destroyer, comes suddenly. What is to be done? Except resorting to the two feet of the destroyer of cupid (Śiva) there is no other recourse.

महेश्वरे वा जगतामधीश्वरे
जनार्दने वा जगदन्तरात्मनि।
तयोर्न भेदप्रतिपत्तिरस्ति मे
तथापि भक्तिस्तरुणेन्दुशेखरे॥८४॥

Between Maheśvara and the Lord of the worlds and Janārdana, and the pervading Spirit of the universe, I have no conception of any difference; still I am strongly drawn to the young-moon-crested God.

स्फुरत्स्फारज्योत्स्नाधवलिततले क्वापि पुलिने
सुखासीनाः शान्तध्वनिषु रजनीषु द्युसरितः।
भवाभोगोद्विग्नाः शिव शिव शिवेत्युच्चवचसा
कदा यास्यामोऽन्तर्गतबहुलबाष्पाकुलदृशः॥८५॥

On nights when all sounds are hushed up, sitting at ease somewhere on the sandy bank of the heavenly river, the surface of which (bank) is whitened by the brilliant flood of moonlight, and grown despondent on account of the wearisomeness of worldly existence, when shall we, loudly uttering the words "Śiva, Śiva!" have our eyes flooded with copious tears proceeding from supreme bliss!

वितीर्णे सर्वस्वे तरुणकरुणापूर्णहृदयाः
स्मरन्तः संसारे विगुणपरिणामा विधिगतीः।
कदा पुण्यारण्ये परिणतशरच्चन्द्रकिरणां-
स्त्रियामां नेष्यामो हरचरणचित्तैकशरणाः॥८६॥

When shall we spend in holy forests nights bright with a full-Moon, thinking solely of Hara's blessed feet and relying on them as the sole refuge, having given away all that we had to the poor, with hearts full of compassions, remembering the cruel and strange happenings and vicissitudes by cruel Fate!

कदा वाराणस्याममरतटिनीरोधसि वस-
न्वसानः कौपीनं शिरसि निदधानोऽञ्जलिपुटम्।
अये गौरीनाथ त्रिपुरहर शम्भो त्रिनयन
प्रसीदेत्याक्रोशन्निमिषमिव नेष्यामि दिवसान्॥८७॥

When shall I, wearing a small strip of cloth, and residing in Vārāṇasī on the bank of the river of gods, pass my days like a moment crying out–"have mercy, oh Lord of Gaurī, destroyer of the three cities, Oh Saṁbhu, oh three-eyed God!, having placed on my head my folded palms!"

स्नात्वा गाङ्गैः पयोभिः शुचिकुसुमफलैरर्चयित्वा विभो त्वां
ध्येये ध्यानं नियोज्य क्षितिधरकुहरग्रावपर्यङ्कमूले।
आत्मारामोऽफलाशी गुरुवचनरतस्त्वत्प्रसादात्स्मरारे
दुःखं मोक्ष्ये कदाहं समकरचरणे पुंसि सेवासमुत्थम्॥८८॥

Having bathed in the waters of the Gaṅgā, and worshipped you, O Lord, with fruits and flowers undefiled, and having tied my attention, sitting on a stony cauch in the gorge of a mountain, on you, the object of contemplation, when shall I, O Enemy of Smara, be free by your grace, from the pain of serving a master having hands and feet just like myself, delightfully carrying the words of the preceptor, living on fruits (only) and self-complacent.

एकाकी निःस्पृहः शान्तः पाणिपात्रो दिगम्बरः।
कदा शम्भो भविष्यामि कर्मनिर्मूलनक्षमः॥८९॥

O Śaṁbhu! When shall I, living all alone, be free from

desire and be peaceful, and having for my pot my hand (only) and for my garments the quarters, be able to root out *Karma*?

पाणिं पात्रयतां निसर्गशुचिना भैक्षेण संतुष्यतां
यत्र क्वापि निषीदतां बहुतृणं विश्वं मुहुः पश्यताम्।
अत्यागेऽपि तनोरखण्डपरमानन्दावबोधस्पृशा-
मध्वा कोऽपि शिवप्रसादसुलभः संपत्स्यते योगिनाम्॥९०॥

Those, who make their palms their eating bowls; satisfy with the God-given alms pure and pious; sit somewhere viewing like a fibre the universe on and on, and touch the supreme safisfaction of the self; on those sages be bestowed by grace of Śiva, the effable, easy path of salvation.

कौपीनं शतखण्डजर्जरतरं कन्था पुनस्तादृशी
निश्चिन्तं सुखसाध्यभैक्षमशनं शय्या श्मशाने वने।
मित्रामित्रसमानता पशुपतेश्चिन्ताऽथ शून्यालये
ध्वस्ताशेषमदप्रमादमुदितो योगी सुखं तिष्ठति॥९१॥

A small ragged piece for *kaupīna*, a very ragged upper cloth for protection from cold, freedom from all care, a life of a beggar content with any *Bhikṣā* doled out without asking, lying down for sleep in the burning ground or in the forest, independent and unrestrained movements, being no servant or slave to any one, a mind always perfectly tranquil, firmness and steadiness in the blissful yoga abstractions,-when all these are in hand, what is sovereignty over the three worlds worth?

ब्रह्माण्डमण्डलीमात्रं किं लोभाय मनस्विनः।
शफरीस्फुरितेनाब्धिः क्षुब्धो न खलु जायते॥९२॥

Would even the whole of the cosmic circle be a temptation to a man of tranquil mind? Would the ocean be agitated by the jumping and fast movements of fishes?

मातर्लक्ष्मि भजस्व कंचिदपरं मत्काङ्क्षिणी मा स्म भू-
र्भोगेभ्यः स्पृहयालवो न हि वयं का निःस्पृहाणामसि।
सद्यःस्यूतपलाशपत्रपुटिकापात्रे पवित्रीकृतै-
र्भिक्षासक्तुभिरेव संप्रति वयं वृत्तिं समीहामहे॥९३॥

Mother wealth, follow someone else, do not be longing for

me. We have no eagerness for enjoyments. What are you to us who are free from desires? Now we wish to subsist on barley grain collected by begging in a purified vessel made of *Palāśa* leaves joined together on the spot.

महीं रम्या शय्या विपुलमुपधानं भुजलता
वितानं चाकाशं व्यजनमनुकूलोऽयमनिलः।
स्फुरद्दीपश्चन्द्रो विरतिवनितासङ्गमुदितः
सुखं शान्तः शेते मुनिरतनुभूतिर्नृप इव॥९४॥

Like a king possessed by no means small wealth an ascetic with ashes besmeared (to his body) and peaceful mind sleeps quietly, delighted in the company of woman *viz.* indifference, the earth being to him a delightful bed, his creeper-like arm a spacious pillow, the sky his canopy, the favourable breeze and the moon a brilliant lamp.

भिक्षाशी जनमध्यसङ्गरहितः स्वायत्तचेष्टः सदा
दानादानविरक्तमार्गनिरतः कश्चित्तपस्वी स्थितः।
रथ्याकीर्णविशीर्णजीर्णवसनैरास्युतकन्थाधरो
निर्मानो निरहंकृतिः शमसुखाभोगैकबद्धस्पृहः॥९५॥

There is an ascetic, living on alms, free from attachment in the midst of the people, his movements are under his control, he is attached to the path which is free from giving and taking, wearing a wallet made of old threadbare clothes thrown away in the streets, not caring for honour, not proud, and wishing solely for the enjoyment of tranquil pleasure.

चाण्डालः किमयं द्विजातिरथवा शूद्रोऽथ किं तापसः
किं वा तत्त्वविवेकपेशलमतिर्योगीश्वरः कोऽपि किम्।
इत्युत्पन्नविकल्पजल्पमुखरैः संभाष्यमाणा जनै-
र्न क्रुद्धाः पथि नैव तुष्टमनसो यान्ति स्वयं योगिनः॥९६॥

When accosted by people who loquacious express doubt and surmise, such as "Is he a *Cāṇḍāla*, or a twice-born or a Sūdra, or an ascetic, or a supreme Yogi with his mind full of discrimination of Reality," the Yogis themselves go on their way neither being pleased nor being displeased in mind.

हिंसाशून्यमयत्नलभ्यमशनं धात्रा मरुत्कल्पितं
व्यालानां पशवस्तृणाङ्कुरभुजः सृष्टा स्थलीशायिनः।
संसारार्णवलङ्घनक्षमधियां वृत्तिः कृता सा नृणां
यामन्वेषयतां प्रयान्ति सततं सर्वे समाप्तिं गुणाः॥९७॥

The creator ordained the air to serve the serpents as food not involving the sin of destroying life, and accessible without any effort; animals living on land be made to eat grass; (but) to men, whose talents are capable of bearing them over the ocean of life, he has assigned such a living that while in pursuit of it all their good qualities are invariably brought to an end.

गंगातीरे हिमगिरिशिलाबद्धपद्मासनस्य
ब्रह्मध्यानाभ्यसनविधिना योगनिद्रां गतस्य।
किं तैर्भाव्यं मम सुदिवसैर्यत्र ते निर्विशङ्काः
कण्डूयन्ते जरठहरिणा स्वाङ्गमङ्गे मदीये॥९८॥

Would I ever see those lucky days when I were beside the Gaṅgā, on the slopes of the Himālayas seated in *padmāsana* in yoga exercise regular gone into the magnetic sleep in the pleasure of knowing the supreme self while the wild hogs fearlessly rub against me their itchy bodies?

पाणिः पात्रं पवित्रं भ्रमणपरिगतं भैक्षमक्षय्यमन्नं
विस्तीर्णं वस्त्रमाशादशकमपमलं तल्पमस्वल्पमूर्वी।
येषां निःसङ्गतान्तःकरणपरिणतस्वात्मसंतोषिणस्ते
धन्याः संन्यस्तदैन्यव्यतिकरनिकराः कर्म निर्मूलयन्ति॥९९॥

The hand is the holy *Bhikṣā* receiving vessel, the *bhikṣā* is got from a numbei of houses by walking in the streets. The food so got is immortal *anna*. The covering cloth is the sky of ten directions of infinite length and breadth. The bed is the widest of earth absolutely free from any shaking or fear of falling down. Those blessed men devoid of any attachments and desires and for the very reason enjoying maximum of joy, rising and flowing in their heart, uproot entirely all *saṁsāra* and maintain their self-respect and independence totally avoiding the least compromising of their independence and self-respect.

मातर्मेदिनि तात मारुत सखे तेजः सुबन्धो जल
भ्रातर्व्योम निबद्ध एव भवतामेष प्रणामाञ्जलिः।
युष्मत्संगवशोपजातसुकृतोद्रेकस्फुरन्निर्मल-
ज्ञानापास्तसमस्तमोहमहिमा लीये परे ब्रह्मणि॥१००॥

Oh Earth! my mother! oh wind, my father! Oh Fire, my friend! oh water, my good relative! Oh Sky, my brother! Here is my last salutation to you with clasped hands! Having cast away infatuation with its wonderful power, by means of an amplitude of pure knowledge resplendent with merits enveloped through my association with you all, I now merge in the Supreme Brahman.

EXTRA VERSES

परिचरितव्याः सन्तो यद्यपि कथयन्ति नो सदुपदेशम्।
यास्त्वेषां स्वैरकथास्ता एव भवन्ति शास्त्राणि॥१॥

Good men should be served though they do not give good advice. For what come from them as random discourses serve as rules for guidance.

भिक्षा कामदुघा धेनुः कन्था शीतनिवारिणी।
अचला तु शिवे भक्तिर्विभवैः किं प्रयोजनम्॥२॥

Charity is a cow that yields all desires; a wallet protects from cold; my devotion to Śiva is firm; what then is the need of riches?

किं तेन हेमगिरिणा रजताद्रिणा वा
यत्राश्रिताश्च तरवस्तरवस्त एव।
मन्यामहे मलयमेव यदाश्रयेण
कंकोलनिंबकुटजा अपि चन्दनाः स्युः॥३॥

What profit is there in the mountain of gold (Meru) or in that of silver (Kailāsa) where the trees that grow remain the same trees (without any change). We honour the Malaya alone, because by its contact even the Kaṅkola, the Nimba, and the Kutaja trees acquire the fragrance of sandal trees.

शैय्या शैलशिला गृहं गिरिगुहा वस्त्रं तरूणां त्वचः
सारङ्गाः सुहृदो ननु क्षितिरुहां वृत्तिः फलैः कोमलैः।
येषां नैर्झरमम्बुपानमुचितं रत्यै च विद्याङ्गना
मन्ये ते परमेश्वराः शिरसि यैर्बद्धो न सेवाञ्जलिः॥४॥

I consider those men to be supremely rich, who have never joined their plams overhead in token of submission, to whom a slab on some mountain is as a couch and a cave in mountain as a home, to whom the barks of trees are as raiment and dear as friends, whose subsistence is by the sweet fruits of trees, who find an aggreable beverage in spring water, and to whom learning is as a pleasure giving consort.

सत्यामेव त्रिलोकीसरिति हरशिरश्चुम्बिनीविच्छटायां
सद्वृत्तिं कल्पयन्त्यां तटविटपिभवैर्वल्कलैः सत्फलैश्च।
कोऽयं विद्वान्विपत्तिज्वरजनितरुजातीव दुःखासिकानां
वक्त्रं वीक्षेत दुःस्थे यदि हि न विभृयात्स्वे कुटुम्बेऽनुकम्पाम्॥५॥

When there is the river of the three worlds, the lustre of whose waist garment touches the head of Śiva, and which with good fruits and with the barks of the trees lining its bank furnishes a splendid living, what wise man is there, who, with the intense pain from barrowing miseries, if he had no commiseration for his ill-placed family?

उद्यानेषु विचित्रभोजनविधिस्तीव्रातितीव्रं तपः
कौपीनावरणं सुवस्त्रममितं भिक्षाटनं मण्डनम्।
आसन्नं मरणं च मङ्गलसमं यस्यां समुत्पद्यते
तां काशीं परिहृत्य हन्त विबुधैरन्यत्र किं स्थीयते॥६॥

Alas! Why do wise men live elsewhere, rejecting Kāsī where the most regorous penance as varied dinners is given in gardens, where a strip of cloth to cover the body is decent raiment, where the glory is an unlimited wandering for alms, and where approaching death is like a blessing.

नायं ते समयो रहस्यमधुना निद्राति नाथो यदि
स्थित्वा द्रक्ष्यति कुप्यति प्रभुरिति द्वारेषु येषां वचः।
चेतस्तानपहाय याहि भवनं देवस्य विश्वेषितु-
र्निर्दौवारिकनिर्दयोक्त्यपरुषं निःसीमशर्मप्रदम्॥७॥

Oh heart! leaving those at whose doors you hear such words as "this is not the time for you (to see the master)", "now he is in private", "the master is asleep"; if he were to see you waiting he will get angry" go to the abode of that lord who is the ruler of the universe–an abode which gives unlimited felicity, and whose doors are free from all these harsh words of the guards.

अनावर्ती कालो व्रजति स वृथा तन्न गणितं
दशास्तास्ताः सोढा व्यसनशतसंपातविधुराः।
कियद्वा वक्ष्यामः किमिव बत नात्मन्यपकृतं
त्वया यावत्तावत्पुनरपि तदेव व्यवसितम्॥८॥

"Time never returns; it passes uselessly"–a fact which was never considered by you; you accommodated yourself to the various conditions, which are adverse on account of the concurrence of a hundred difficulties; or what shall we say? What harm have you done yourself? Every now and then you have been repeatedly doing the same.

उत्तिष्ठ क्षणमेकमुद्वह गुरुं दारिद्र्यभारं सखे
श्रान्तस्तावदहं चिरं मरणजं सेवे त्वदीयं सुखम्।
इत्युक्तो धनवर्जितेन सहसा गत्वा स्मशाने शवो
दारिद्र्यान्मरणं वरं वरमिति ज्ञात्वैव तूष्णीं स्थितः॥९॥

"Get up, oh friend! and bear the heavy load of poverty for a moment. I am now fatigued. So let me enjoy for a long time the happiness from death which you have." Thus was a corpse addressed by a penniless fellow who had hurried to the cemetery, but it remained silent as it was well aware that death was far better than penury.

एता हसन्ति च रुदन्ति च कार्यहेतो-
र्विश्वासयन्ति च परं न च विश्वसन्ति।
तस्मान्नरेण कुलशीलसमन्वितेन
नार्यः श्मशानघटिका इव वर्जनीयाः॥१०॥

The women laugh and cry as it suits their purpose; make others confide in them but they themselves do not confide. Therefore a man possessed of nobility of birth and character should abandon women as one rejects jars in a cemetery.

कार्कश्यं स्तनयोर्दृशोस्तरलताऽलीकं मुखे श्लाघ्यते
कौटिल्यं कचसंचये प्रवचने मान्द्यं त्रिके स्थूलता।
भीरुत्वं हृदये सदैव कथितं मायाप्रयोगः प्रिये
यासां दोषगणो गुणो मृगदृशां ताः स्युः पशूनां प्रियाः॥११॥

The brutes alone would be dear to those fawn-eyed women in whose case demerits are merits for their hardness of breasts, unsteadiness of the eyes, and falsehood on the tongue are praised, crookedness of hair, dulness of the face, and plumpness of the hips, are commended; and timidity of the heart and deceitful tricks towards their beloved always mentioned with approbation.

क्वचिद्वीणावाद्यं क्वचिदपि च हाहेति रुदितं
क्वचिद्विद्गोष्ठी क्वचिदपि सुरामत्तकलहः।
क्वचिद्रामा रम्याः क्वचिदपि गलत्कुष्ठवपुषो
न जाने संसारः किममृतमयः किं विषमयः॥१२॥

In some places, there is playing on the Vīṇā while in others are wailings of lamentations; in some places there are learned conversations, while in others there are drunken brawls; in some places there are pretty damsels, while in others there are those whose bodies are covered with flowing leprous sores. Under these circumstances, I do not know whether worldly life is sweet like nectar or bitter like poison.

गात्रैर्गिरा च विकलश्चटुमीश्वराणां
कुर्वन्नयं प्रहसनस्य नटः कृतोऽसि।
तं त्वां पुनः पलितकर्णकभाजमेनं
नाट्येन केन नटयिष्यति दीर्घमायुः॥१३॥

Deformed in limbs and lisping in speech, here are you that have been made the buffoon of a farce, while flattering; what part (I do not know) will prolonged life make you play, such as you are, with your ears bordered with grey hair.

चला लक्ष्मीश्चलाः प्राणाश्चलं जीवितयौवनम्।
चलाचले च संसारे धर्म एको हि निश्चलः॥१४॥

Wealth is unsteady, so is life, and so is the prime of youth; in this ephemeral worldly career merit alone is firm.

ददतु ददतु गालीर्गालिमन्तो भवन्तो
वयमपि तदभावाद्गलिदानेऽसमर्थाः।
जगति विदितमेतद् 'दीयते विद्यमानं'
न हि शशकविषाणं कोऽपि कस्मै ददाति॥१५॥

You may keep on abusing, since you are possessors of foul language; we are unable to do so, as we do not have a stock of it. It is well-known that whatever is available in the world that can only be given. No one gives to another the horn of a hare.

न भिक्षा दुष्प्रापा पथि मम महारामरचिते
फलैः संपूर्णा भूर्द्विपमृगसुचर्मापि वसनम्।
सुखैर्वा दुःखैर्वा सदृशपरिपाकः खलु यदा
त्रिनेत्रं कस्त्यक्त्वा धनलवमदान्धं प्रणमति॥१६॥

Alms are not unattainable to me in my path lined by rich gardens; the earth is full of fruits, and the skins of deer and the barks of trees serve as raiment; with joys or with sorrows, there is, in fact the same result. Who will then give up the three-eyed God, and bow to the men blinded by pride for a particle of wealth?

नो खड्गप्रविदारिताः करटिनो नोद्वेजिता वैरिण-
स्तन्वङ्ग्या विपुले नितम्बफलके न क्रीडितं लीलया।
नो जुष्टं गिरिराजनिर्झरझणज्झांकारकारं पयः
कालोऽयं परपिण्डलोलुपतया काकैरिव प्रेरितः॥१७॥

With a sword we did not cut asunder elephants; we did not harass our enemies; we did not sip the noisy water of the streamlets of the Himālayas; we passed our time like crows desirous of obtaining a morsel from others.

प्रशान्तशास्त्रार्थविचारचापलं
निवृत्तनानारसकाव्यकौतुकम्।
निरस्तनिःशेषविकल्पविस्तरं
प्रपत्तुमन्विच्छति शंकरं मनः॥१८॥

My mind desires to go to Śaṅkara, for its scruples in the investigation of scriptural meanings being completely set at rest, its delight in poetry full of various sentiments being turned away, and all the different wild doubts being totally dispelled.

भव्यं भुक्तं ततः किं कदशितमथवा वासारान्ते ततः किं
कौपीनं वा ततः किं किमथ सितमहच्चाम्बरं वा ततः किम्।
एका भार्या ततः किं शतगुणगुणिता कोटिरेका ततः किं
त्वेको भ्रान्तस्ततः किं करितुरगशतैर्वेष्टितो वा ततः किम्॥१९॥

What is there if you have eaten excellent rice, or a warse meal at the end of the day? What is there if you have a strip of cloth or a long white garment? What is there if you have one wife, or a number of them endowed with one hundred qualities? And what is there if you wander all alone, or surrounded by hundreds of elephants and horses?

भूः पर्यङ्को निजभुजलता कन्दुकं खं वितानं
दीपश्चन्द्रो विरतिवनितालब्धसङ्गप्रमोदः।
दिक्कान्ताभिः पवनचमरैर्वीज्यमानः समन्ता-
द्भिक्षुः शेते नृप इव भुवि त्यक्तसर्वस्पृहोऽपि॥२०॥

An ascetic, though has abandoned all desires, lies down on the ground like a king, having the earth for his couch, his creeper-like arm for a pillow, the sky for a canopy and the moon for his lamp, experiencing pleasure in his union with the woman called renunciation and fanned from all sides by the attendant maids-the quaters, with their chowries-the winds.

यद्वक्त्रं मुहुरीक्षसे न धनिनां ब्रूषे न चाटुं मृषा
नैषां गर्वगिरः शृणोषि न पुनः प्रत्याशया धावसि।
काले बालतृणानि खादसि सुखं निद्रासि निद्रागमे
तन्मे ब्रूहि कुरंग कुत्र भवता किं नाम तप्तं तपः॥२१॥

Oh antelope! Tell me where and what penance has been performed by you that you have never to see the face of the rich, nor to speak flattering falsehoods, nor to hear their arrogant utterances, nor to run to them with expectation. You eat tender grass when you want and take rest at ease when overtaken by sleep.

समारम्भा भग्नाः कति न कतिवारांस्तव पशो
पिपासोस्तुच्छेऽस्मिन्द्रविणमृगतृष्णार्णवजले।
तथापि प्रत्याशा विरमति न तेऽद्यापि शतधा
न दीर्णं यच्चेतो नियतमशनिग्रावघटितम्॥२२॥

Oh brute! How many and how often have not your efforts in anxiously drinking the despicable waters of the ocean of the mirage of wealth been frustrated, still, your expectation does not abate and as your heart has not yet been broken into hundreds of fragments, it must have verily been made of adamant.

संमोहयन्ति मदयन्ति विडम्बयन्ति
निर्भर्त्सयन्ति रमयन्ति विषादयन्ति।
एताः प्रविश्य सदयं हृदयं नराणां
किं नाम वामनयना न समाचरन्ति॥२३॥

What is it that lovely-eyed women do not do? Having entered the affectionate heart of men they fascinate them, maden them, mock them, despise them, gladden them and cause grief to them.

विवेकव्याकोशे विकसति शमे शाम्यति तृषा-
परिष्वङ्गे तुङ्गे प्रसरतितरां सा परिणतिः।
जराजीर्णैश्वर्यग्रसनगहनाक्षेपकृपण-
स्तृषापात्रं यस्यां भवति मरुतामप्यधिपतिः॥२४॥

When self-restraint developed by discrimination becomes manifest, and when the strong hold of desire is relaxed, there appears that perfection wherein even the lord of gods, becomes an object of pity, wretched on account of the strong distraction caused by the enjoyment of greatness worn out of age.

पुरा विद्वत्तासीदुपशमवतां क्लेशहतये
गता कालेनासौ विषयसुखसिद्ध्यै विषयिणाम्।
इवानीं तु प्रेक्ष्य क्षितितलभुजः शास्त्रविमुखा-
नहो कष्टं सापि प्रतिदिनमधोऽधः प्रविशति॥२५॥

Formerely learning was a means to remove the pain of

those who possessed self-restraint. In course of time it came to be used for securing sensual happiness by sensualists. Seeing that the rulers of the earth are now averse to learning, alas! it is going down and down everyday.

शशिदिवाकरयोर्ग्रहपीडनं
गजभुजंगमयोरपि बन्धनम्।
मतिमतां च विलोक्य दरिद्रतां
विधिरहो बलवानिति मे मतिः॥२६॥

When I see the sun and the moon, the assaults of the demon (Rāhu), behold the bonds of the elephant and the serpent, when I find the wise in poverty, then the thought strikes me – how powerful is fate!

अतिक्रान्तः कालो लटभललनाभोगसुभगो
भ्रमन्तः श्रान्ताः स्मः सुचिरमिह संसारसरणौ।
इदानीं स्वःसिन्धोस्तटभुवि समाक्रन्दनगिरः
सुतारैः फूत्कारैः शिव शिव शिवेति प्रतनुमः॥२७॥

The time (that was) happy on account of the enjoyment of lovely women is passed; and having, for long, wandered along this avenue of the world we are exhausted; now (stationed) on the bank of the Gaṅgā we send forth with deep sighs the cries of invocation with the words-Śiva, Śiva, Śiva.

महादेवो देवः सरिदपि च सैवामरसरि-
द्गुहा एवागारं वसनमपि ता एव हरितः।
सुहृद्वा कालोऽयं व्रतमिदमदैन्यव्रतमिति
कियद्वा वक्ष्यामो वटविटप एवास्तु दयिता॥२८॥

Mahādeva is the God and the stream of the gods (the Gaṅgā) alone is the stream (for me); caves are (my) abode, and even the quarters are (my) raiment; the Destroyer is as a friend; and my own-such conduct (as is) free from meanness; why say more, Let me be wedded to the *Vaṭa* tree alone.

अहो धन्याः केचित्त्रुटितभवबन्धव्यतिकरा
वनान्तेऽचिवन्तो विषमविषयाशीविषगतिम्।
शरच्चन्द्रज्योत्स्नाधवलगगनाभोगसुभगां
नयन्ते ये रात्रिं सुकृतचयचितैकशरणाः॥२९॥

Ah! Fortunate are some who having crushed calamities in the shape of ties for this world and set their hearts only on the acquisition of merits without minding the course of worldly objects which are like dangerous snakes, spend in a forest the night beautiful on account of the refulgent light of the autumnal moon bathing the expanse of the sky.

पत्रं नैव यदा करीरविटपे दोषो वसन्तस्य किं
नोलूकोऽप्यवलोकते यदि दिवा सूर्यस्य किं दूषणम्।
धारा नैव पतन्ति चातकमुखे मेघस्य किं दूषणं
यत्पूर्वं विधिना ललाटलिखितं तन्मार्जितुं कः क्षमः॥३०॥

Is it the fault of spring that there are no leaves on the Karīra? If the owl cannot see in day is it the fault of the sun? What fault is it of the cloud that the current of rain-water does not fall into the mouth of the Cātaka. Who can wipe off that what is already written on the forehead by the creator?

यूयं वयं वयं यूयमित्यासीन्मतिरावयोः।
किं जातमधुना येन यूयं यूयं वयं वयम्॥३१॥

Our view was that you were we and we were you; what has happened now by which you are you and we are we.

जीर्णा कन्था ततः किं सितममलवरं पट्टवस्त्रं ततः किं
एका भार्या ततः किं हयकरिसुगणैरावृतो वा ततः किम्।
भक्तं भुक्तं ततः किं कदशनमथवा वासरान्ते ततः किं
व्यक्तज्योतिर्न चान्तर्मथितभवभयं वैभवं वा ततः किम्॥३२॥

What is there if one has a threadbare wallet or a spotless white silken cloth? What if one has only one wife or is surrounded by a splendid army of horses and elephants? What if one eats delicious food, or coarse food towards the close of the day?

What if there is not the light of the knowledge of Brahman manifested inside (*i.e.* in the heart) or what is there if the glorification in which the fears of worldly existence is destroyed?

अप्रियवचनदरिद्रैः प्रियवचनाढ्यैः स्वदारपरितुष्टैः।
परपरिवादनिवृत्तैः क्वचिन्मण्डिता वसुधा॥३३॥

Leave aside the question whether a man, wounded while facing the enemy attain victory or heaven; the applause of both the armies is, indeed, intensely gratifying to the war.

मालतीकुसुमस्येव द्वे गती ह मनस्विनः।
मूर्ध्नि वा सर्वलोकस्य शीर्यते वन एव वा॥३४॥

High-souled persons have, like the Mālatī flower, two ways either to be at the head of all men, or to fade away in a forest.

कमठकुलाचलदिग्गजफणिपतिविधृतापि चलति वसुधेयम्।
प्रतिपन्नममलमनसां न लति पुंसां युगान्तेऽपि॥३५॥

The earth though supported by the tortoise Kamaṭha, the Kulācala mountains, the *Diggaja* elephants, and the serpent Śeṣa, shakes; but whatever is undertaken by the pureminded remains unchanged even at the end of a *yuga*.

एको देवः केशवो वा शिवो वा
एकं मित्रं भूपतिर्वा यतिर्वा।
एको वासः पत्तने वा वने वा
एका भार्या सुन्दरी वा दरी वा॥३६॥

Choose but one divinity either Keśava or Śiva, one friend either a king or an ascetic, one place of residence – a mansion or a forest, one companion in life, a handsome woman or a mountain valley.

उदन्वच्छिन्ना भूः स च निधिरपां योजनशतं
सदा पान्थः पूषा गगनपरिमाणं कलयति।
इति प्रायो भावाः स्फुरदवधिमुद्रामुकुलिताः
सतां प्रज्ञोन्मेषः पुनरयमसीमा विजयते॥३७॥

The earth is bounded by the ocean, that expanse of waters

again is but a hundred *yojanas*, the sun always takes the measure of the sky by his course. Thus are objects generally limited within distinct boundary marks, but it is the brilliancy of intelect of the wise that is unlimited.

इयत्येतस्मिन्वा निरवधिचमत्कृत्यतिशये
वराहो वा राहुः प्रभवति चमत्कारविषयः।
महोमेको मग्नां यदयमवहद्धन्त सलिले
शिरः शेषः शत्रुं निगलति परः संत्यजति च॥३८॥

In all this collection of exceedingly wonderful things of this nature, or of such extent, either Varāha or Rāhu, pre-eminently stands out as an object of wonder; in that he alone bore up the earth when it was sunk in water; the latter, the head-remnant, in that he swallows his enemy (the sun), and afterwards throws him out.

अभिमुखनिहतस्य सतः
तिष्ठतु तावज्जयोऽथवा स्वर्गः।
उभयबलसाधुवादः
श्रवणसुखोऽसौ बतात्यर्थम्॥३९॥

Let alone the fact that a man killed in the front-ranks in a battle obtains victory or heaven; he must obtain the eulogy of both sides which is exceedingly pleasing to the ear.

अग्राह्यं हृदयं यथैव वदनं यद्दर्पणान्तर्गतं
भावः पर्वतसूक्ष्ममार्गविषमः स्त्रीणां न विज्ञायते।
चित्तं पुष्करपत्रतोयतरलं विद्वद्भिराशंसितं
नारी नाम विषाङ्कुरैरिव लता दोषैः समं वर्धिता॥४०॥

The heart of the woman is as impossible to be cought as the image of the face in a mirror, her feelings cannot be ascertained since they are as difficult as the narrow defile of a mountain, her mind is said by the wise to be as fickle as the water on a lotus-leaf. She grows with her blemishes like a creeper with poisonous sprouts and is known as woman.

रे कन्दर्प करं कदर्थयसि किं कोदण्डटङ्कारितैः
रे रे कोकिल कोमलैः कलरवैः किं त्वं वृथा जल्पसि।
मुग्धे स्निग्धविदग्धमुग्धमधुरैर्लोलैः कटाक्षैरलं
चेतश्चुम्बितचन्द्रचूडचरणध्यानामृतं वर्तते॥४१॥

Why do you, O God of love! trouble your hand with the twangings of your bow? Why do you, O cuckoo! Chatter ineffectually with your soft and sweet notes? O young women! Enough of your glances, affectionate, artful, charming, sweet and unsteady; our heart has fasted the nectar-like contemplation of the moon-crested God.

स्वादिष्टं मधुनो घृताश्च रसवद्यत्प्रस्त्रवत्यक्षरं
दैवी वागमृतात्मनो रसवतस्तेनैव तृप्ता वयम्।
कुक्षौ यावदिमे भवन्ति धृतये भिक्षाहृताः सक्तव-
स्तावदास्यकृतार्जनैर्न हि धनैर्वृत्तिं समीहामहे॥४२॥

We are quite content with those delicious utterances sweeter than honey or clarified butter which the Divine speech sends forth from its ambrosial and immortal body; as long as there is, under our arm, a quantity of barley-meal procurred by begging for our maintenace, so long we do not wish to live on wealth acquired by servitude.

स्थितिः पुण्येऽरण्ये सह परिचयो हन्त हरिणैः
फलैर्मेध्या वृत्तिः प्रतिनदि च तल्पानि दृषदः।
इतीयं सामग्री भवति हरभक्तिं स्पृहयतां
वनं वा गेहं वा सदृशमुपशान्त्यैकमनसाम्॥४३॥

Residence in a sacred forest, in association with the deer, sacred maintenance of fruits, stones for couches on the bank of every river-such are the materials for those who like to offer devotion to God. To those whose minds are fixed on renunciation alone, whether they live in a house or a forest, it is all the same.

वरं पर्वतदुर्गेषु भ्रान्तं वनचरैः सह।
न मूर्खजनसंपर्कः सुरेन्द्रभवनेष्वपि॥४४॥

It is better to wander in company of foresters through the

inaccessible regions of mountains than to have relations with fools even in the halls of Surendra, the Lord of gods.

सिंहो बली द्विरदशूकरमांसभोजी
संवत्सरेण रतिमेति किलैकवारम्।
पारावतः खरशिलाकणमात्रभोजी
कामी भवत्यनुदिनं वद कोऽत्र हेतुः॥४५॥

A lion, strong and living on the flesh of elephants and hogs, ruts once in a year. The dove, eating only hard pebbles, ruts daily. Say what is the cause of it?

साहित्यसङ्गीतकलाविहीनः
साक्षात्पशुः पुच्छविषाणहीनः।
तृणं न खादन्नपि जीवमान–
स्तद्भागधेयं परमं पशूनाम्॥४६॥

A person, unacquainted with literature, music and the arts, is in fact, a beast without horns and tail; and it is the highest piece of good luck for beasts that he lives without eating grass.

सूनुः सच्चरितः सती प्रियतमा स्वामी प्रसादोन्मुखः
स्निग्धं मित्रमवञ्चकः परिजनो निष्क्लेशलेशं मनः।
आकारो रुचिरः स्थिरश्च विभवो विद्यावदातं मुखं
तुष्टे विष्टपकष्टहारिणि हरौ संप्राप्यते देहिना॥४७॥

A well-conducted son, a devoted wife, a liberal master, a loving friend, an honest servant, a mind free from the least of anxiety, a handsome form, abiding riches, a mouth purified by learning can be gained by a man when the Lord, the destroyer of the troubles of the world, is pleased.

तानीन्द्रियाणि सकलानि तदेव कर्म
सा बुद्धिरप्रतिहता वचनं तदेव।
अर्थोष्मणा विरहितः पुरुषः स एव
त्वन्यः क्षणेन भवतीति विचित्रमेतत्॥४८॥

All these organs are the same, action is the same, intellect is the same, speech is the same, that man, though he is the same, becomes quite a different person at the moment he is deprived of the warmth of wealth. This is indeed wonderful.

रे रे चातक सावधानमनसा मित्र क्षणं श्रूयता-
मम्भोदा बहवो हि सन्ति गगने सर्वेऽपि नैतादृशाः।
केचिद्वृष्टिभिरार्द्रयन्ति वसुधां गर्जन्ति केचिद्वृथा
यं यं पश्यसि तस्य तस्य पुरतो मा ब्रूहि दीनं वचः॥४९॥

Oh friend Cātaka! Listen attentively for a moment to what I say. There are no doubt numerous clouds in the sky, but all are not such as you expect them to be. Some wet the earth by their showers, while others make only an useless noise; so do not say anything miserable before everyone that you may chance to meet.

त्वमेव चातकाधार इति केषां न गोचरः।
किमम्भोदवरास्माकं कार्पण्योक्तिं प्रतीक्षसे॥५०॥

O magnanimous cloud! Who does not know that you alone are the supporter of the cātakas? Why do you then wait for our plaintive appeal?

को न याति वशं लोके मुखे पिण्डेन पूरितः।
मृदङ्गो मुखलेपेन करोति मधुरध्वनिम्॥५१॥

Who, in this world, does not become submissive when his mouth is filled with a morsel? A mṛdaṅga gives out a sweet sound when its face is coated with dough.

क्षुद्राः सन्ति सहस्त्रशः स्वभरणव्यापारमात्रोद्यताः
स्वार्थो यस्य परार्थ एव स पुमानेकः सतामग्रणीः।
दुष्पूरोदरपूरणाय पिबति स्त्रोतःपतिं वाडवो
जीमूतस्तु निदाघसंभृतजगत्संतापविच्छित्तये॥५२॥

There are thousands of mean fellows who are only busy in filling their bellies. He only is the leader of the good who counts the interest of others as his own interest. The submarine fire consumes the waters of the ocean to fill his belly which is difficult of being satiated, while the cloud destroys the accumulated heat of the summer which tortures the whole world.

दूरादर्थं घटयति नवं दूरतश्चापशब्दं
त्यक्त्वा भूयो भवति निरतः सत्सभारञ्जनेषु।
मन्दं मन्दं रचयति पदं लोकचित्तानुवृत्त्या
कामं मन्त्री कविरिव सदा खेदभारैरमुक्तः॥५३॥

A minister, who brings together new meanings and altogether avoids all offensive expressions, devotes himself to the task of pleasing the good, and gradually takes every forward move in consonance with the feelings of the people, is thus never free from the burden of troubles like a poet who brings about new meanings, avoids incorrect words, strives to please the learned and slowly compiles poems which would be attractive to the people.

रक्तत्वं कमलानां सत्पुरुषाणां परोपकारित्वम्।
असतां च निर्दयत्वं स्वभावसिद्धं त्रिषु त्रितयम्॥५४॥

Redness in lotuses, beneficence in good men and ruthlessness in the wicked-these three are by nature established respectively in the three.

येषां न विद्या न तपो न दानं
ज्ञानं न शीलं न गुणो न धर्मः।
ते मर्त्यलोके भुवि भारभूता
मनुष्यरूपेण मृगाश्चरन्ति॥५५॥

Those who do not have education, practice of penance, knowledge, character, virtue or religious merit, they roam in the mortal world as beasts in a human form in the earth.

यन्नागा मदवारिभिन्नकरटास्तिष्ठन्ति निद्रालसा
द्वारे हेमविभूषणाश्च तुरगा वल्गन्ति यद्दर्पिताः।
वीणावेणुमृदङ्गशङ्खपटहैः सुप्तस्तु यद्बोध्यते
तत्सर्वं सुरलोकदेवसदृशं धर्मस्य विस्फूर्जितम्॥५६॥

Elephants, whose temples have burst through rut and who are heavy with sleep, stand at the gate, as well as highspirited horses adorned with golden ornaments prance there, (and their owner) is awakened from his sleep by the sound of the lute, the life, the drum, the conchshell and *eymbals* : all this a state like that of the Lord of the gods–is the manifestation of the power of religious merit.

वचो हि सत्यं परमं विभूषणं
गजाङ्गनायाः कृशता कटौ च।
द्विजस्य विद्यैव पुनस्तथा क्षमा
शीलं हि सर्वस्य नरस्य भूषणम्॥५७॥

Truthfulness is the best ornament, slender waist in a woman of the Hastinī class, and learning as well as is an ornament in a Brahmin. Every one is best adorned by a virtuous conduct.

यदा योगाभ्यासव्यसनकृशयोरात्ममनसो-
रविच्छिन्ना मैत्री स्फुरति कृतिनस्तस्य किमु तैः।
प्रियाणामालापैरधरमधुभिर्वक्त्रविधुभिः
सनिश्वासामोदैः सकुचकलशाश्लेषसुरतैः॥५८॥

When a good man engaging himself in the practice of yoga, has his intelligence and mind well-restrained and the sweet feeling of love to all humanity is sweetly flowing in the heart, why should he care for the pleasant talk of women or the honey of their lips or their moon like face or their sweetly fragrant breath or their amorous sports with embraces of pot like breasts.

कार्यायत्तं फलं पुंसां बुद्धिः कर्मानुसारिणी।
तथापि सुधिया भाव्यं सुविचार्यैव कुर्वता॥५९॥

The fruit which men get depends on action, and the inducement to action is in consonance with it, still a wise man should undertake an action only after mature consideration.

को लाभो गुणिसंगमः किमसुखं प्राज्ञेतरैः संगतिः
का हानिः समयच्युतिर्निपुणता का धर्मतत्वे रतिः।
कः शूरो विजितेन्द्रियः प्रियतमा कानुव्रता किं धनं
विद्या किं सुखमप्रवासगहनं राज्यं किमाज्ञाफलम्॥६०॥

What is a gain? Company of the virtuous. What is trouble? Company of fools. What is loss? Letting slip an opportunity.

What is vigilance? Devoted application to the principle of righteousness. Who is valiant? He who has subdued his passions. Who is the best beloved? The faithful wife. What is wealth? Learning. What is happiness? Not going out on travels. What is royalty? The power to command.

एकेनापि हि शूरेण पादाक्रान्तं महीतलम्।
क्रियते भास्करेणेव स्फारस्फुरिततेजसा॥६१॥

As by the sun of profusely glittering splendour, so by a warrior, though single handed, the entire surface of the earth is overpowered with his *pādas* (feet *i.e.* power; rays in case of the Sun).

अकिञ्चनस्य दान्तस्य शान्तस्य समचेतसः।
सदा सन्तुष्टमनसः सर्वाः सुखमया दिशः॥६२॥

All quarters are full of happiness to him, who possesses nothing, but is self-restrained, calm, preserves an equilibrium of mind and is always contented at heart.

APPENDIX - I

विज्ञानशतकम्

विगलदमलदानश्रेणिसौरभ्यलोभो-
पगतमधुपमालाव्याकुलाकाशदेशः।
अवतु जगदशेषं शश्वदुग्रात्मदर्पो
विपुलपरिधिदन्तोद्दण्डशुण्डो गणेशः॥१॥

यत्सत्तया सदिदमस्ति यदात्मभासा
प्रद्योतितं जगदशेषमपास्तदोषम्।
तद्ब्रह्म निष्कलमसंगमपारसौख्यं
प्रत्यग्भजे परममङ्गलमद्वितीयम्॥२॥

हे पुत्रा व्रजताभयं यत इतो गेहं जनन्या समं
रागद्वेषमदादयो भवतु वः पन्थाः शिवो मायया।
काशीं साम्प्रतमागतोऽहमहह क्लेन हातुं वपुः
सर्वानर्थगृहं सुपर्वतटिनीवीचिश्रिया मण्डिताम्॥३॥

तीर्थावस्थानजन्यं न भवति सुकृतं दुष्कृतोन्मूलनं वा
यस्मादाभ्यां विहीनः श्रुतिसमधिगतप्रत्यगात्मा जनानाम्।
सर्वेषामद्वितीयो निरतिशयसुखो यद्यपि स्वप्रकाशा-
स्तीर्थे विद्यास्तथापि स्पृहयति तपसे यत्तदाश्चर्यहेतुः॥४॥

प्रज्ञावन्तोऽपि केचिच्चिरमुपनिषदाद्यर्थकारा यतन्तो
व्याकुर्वन्तोऽपि केचिद्दलितपरमता यद्यपि ज्ञाततत्त्वाः।
तीर्थे तीर्थे तथापि भ्रमणरसिकतां नो जहात्यध्वखेदा-
द्यत्तत्कष्टं विधत्ते मम मनसि सदा पश्यतस्तत्र कृत्यम्॥५॥

यावत्ते यमकिंकराः करतलक्रूरासिपाशादयो
दुर्दान्ताः सृणिराजदीर्घसुनखा दंष्ट्राकरालाननाः।
नाकर्षन्ति नरान्धनादिरहितान्यत्तावदिष्टेच्छया
युष्माभिः क्रियतां धनस्य कृपणास्त्यागः सुपर्वादिषु॥६॥

आढ्यः कश्चिदपण्डितोऽपि विदुषां सेव्यः सदा धार्मिका
विश्वेषामुपकारको मृगदृशामानन्दकन्दाकरः।
कर्पूरद्युतिकीर्तिभूषितहरिद्भूमण्डले गीयते
शश्वद्बन्दिजनैर्महीतनुभृतः पुण्यैर्न कस्योदयः॥७॥

यमाराध्याराध्यं त्रिभुवनगुरुं प्राप वसतिं
ध्रुवो ज्योतिश्चक्रे सुचिरमनवद्यां शिशुरपि।
अवापः प्रल्हादः परमपदमाराध्य यमितः
स कस्यालं क्लेशो हरति न हरिः कीर्तितगुणः॥८॥

को देवो भुवनोदभावनकरो विश्वेश्वरो विद्यते
यस्याज्ञावशवर्तिनो जलधयो नाप्लावयन्ति क्षितिम्।
इत्याम्नातमपीश्वरं सुरशिरोरत्नं जगत्साक्षिणं
सर्वज्ञं धनयौवनोद्धतमना नो मन्यते बालिशः॥९॥

कस्येमौ पितरौ मनोभववता तापेन संयोजिता-
वन्योन्यं तनयादिकं जनयतो भूम्यादिभूतात्मभिः।
इत्थं दुःस्थमतिर्मनोभवरतिर्यो मन्यते नास्तिकः
शान्तिस्तस्य कथं भवेद्धनवतो दुष्कर्मधर्माश्रयात्॥१०॥

देहाद्यात्ममतानुसारि भवतां यद्यस्ति मुग्धं मतं
वेदव्यासविनिन्दितं कथमहो पित्राद्यपत्ये तदा।
दाहादिः क्रियते विशुद्धफलको युष्माभिरुद्वेजितैः
शोकेनार्थपरायणैरपसदैर्दृष्टार्थमात्रार्थिभिः॥११॥

विपश्चिद्देहादौ क्वचिदपि ममत्वं न कुरुते
परब्रह्मध्याता गगननगराकारसदृशे।
निरस्ताहंकारः श्रुतिजनितविश्वाससुभगो-
निरातङ्कोऽव्यग्रः प्रकृतिमधुरालापचतुरः॥१२॥

नित्यानित्यपदार्थतत्त्वविषये नित्यं विचारः सतां
संसर्गे मितभाषिता हितमिताहारोऽनहंकारिता।
कारुण्यं कृपणे जने सुखिजने प्रीतिः सदा यस्य सः
प्रायेणैव तपः करोति सुकृती शश्वन्मुकुन्दप्रियः॥१३॥

संसारेऽपि परोपकारकरणख्यातव्रता मानवा
ये संपत्तिगृहा विचारचतुरा विश्वेश्वराराधकाः।
तेऽप्येनं भवसागरं जनिमृतिग्राहाकुलं दुस्तरं
गंभीरं सुतरां तरन्ति विविधव्याध्याधिवीचीमयम्॥१४॥

धन्या एते पुमांसो यदयमहमिति त्यक्तचेतो विकल्पा
निश्शंकं संचरन्तो विदधति मलिनं कर्म कामप्रयुक्ताः।
जानन्तोऽप्यर्थहीनं जगदिदमखिलं भ्रान्तवद् द्वैतजालं
रागद्वेषादिमन्तो वयमयमिति हा न त्यजन्तेऽभिमानम्॥१५॥

न चेत्ते सामर्थ्यं भवनमरणातङ्कहरणे
मनोऽनिर्दिष्टेऽस्मिन्नपगतगुणे ज्ञातुमकले।
तदा मेघश्यामं कमलदलदीर्घाक्षममलं
भजस्व श्रीरङ्गं शरदमृतधामाधिकमुखम्॥१६॥

भ्रातः शान्तं प्रशान्ते क्वचिदपि निपतन्मित्र रे भूधराग्रे
ग्रीष्मे ध्यानाय विष्णोः स्पृहयसि सुतरां निर्विशङ्कं गुहायाम्।
अन्विष्यंस्तादृगत्र क्षितिवलयतले स्थानमुन्मूलयैतत्
संसारानर्थवृक्षं मथितगुरुमहामोहमूलं विशालम्॥१७॥

विश्वेश्वरो भवति विश्वजनीनजन्मा
विश्वंभरे भगवति प्रथितप्रभावे।
यो दत्तचित्तविषयः सुकृती कृतार्थो
यत्र क्वचित्प्रतिदिनं निवसन् गृहादौ॥१८॥

ध्यानव्यग्रं भवतु हृदयं तिष्ठतो यत्र तत्र
श्रीमद्विष्णोस्त्रिभुवनपतेर्नित्यमानन्दमूर्तेः।
लक्ष्मीचेतः कुमुदविपुलानन्दपीयूषधाम्नो
मेघच्छायाप्रतिभटतनोः क्लेशसिन्धुं तितीर्षोः॥१९॥

कामादित्रिकमेव मूलमखिलक्लेशस्य मायोद्भवं
मर्त्यानामिति देवमौलिविलसद् भ्राजिष्णुचूडामणिः।
श्रीकृष्णो भगवानवोचदखिले प्राणप्रियो मत्प्रभु-
र्यस्मात्तत्रिकमुद्यतेन मनसा हेयं पुमर्थार्थिना॥२०॥

कामस्यापि निदानमाहुरपरे मायां महाशासनां
निश्चित्कां सकलप्रपञ्चरचनाचातुर्यलीलावतीम्।
यत्संगाद्भगवानपि प्रभवति प्रत्यङ्महामोहहा
श्रीरङ्गे भुवनोदयावनलयव्यापारचक्रेऽक्रियः॥२१॥

यदध्यस्तं सर्वं स्रजि भुजगवद्भाति पुरतो
महामायोद्गीर्णं गगनपवनाद्य तनुभृताम्।
भवेत्तस्या भ्रान्तेर्मुररिपुरधिष्ठानमुदयं
यतो न स्याद्भ्रान्तिर्निरधिकरणा क्वापि जगति॥२२॥

वियत्पृथ्वीवायुज्वलनजलजं चाखिलमिदं
महामायासङ्गाद्भुजग इव रज्ज्वां भ्रमकरम्।
तदत्यन्ताह्लादं ह्यजरममरं चिन्तय मनः
परब्रह्माव्यग्रं हरिहरसुराद्यैरवगतम्॥२३॥

चिद्रत्नमत्र पतितं वपुरन्धकूपे
पुंसो भ्रमादनुपमं महनीयतेजः।
सद्यः समुद्धरति तद्विविता कृतार्थो
मन्ये स एव समुपासितविश्वनाथः॥२४॥

स्वान्तव्योम्नि निरस्तकल्मषघने सद्बुद्धितारावली-
संदीप्ते समुदेति चेन्निरुपमानन्दप्रभामण्डलः।
ब्रह्मज्ञानसुधाकरः कवलिताविद्यान्धकारस्तदा
क्व व्योम क्व सदागतिः क्व हुतभुक् क्वाम्भः क्व सर्वंसहा॥२५॥

क्वाहं ब्रह्मेति विद्या निरतिशयसुखं दर्शयन्ती विशुद्धं
कूटस्थस्वप्रकाशं प्रकृतिसुचरिता खण्डयन्ती च मायाम्।
क्वाविद्याहंममेति स्थगितपरसुखा चित्तभित्तौ लिखन्ती
सर्वानर्थाननर्थान् विषयगिरिभुवा वासनागैरिकेण॥२६॥

यावज्जागर्ति चित्ते दुरितकलुषिते प्राणिनो वित्तपुत्र-
क्षेत्राद्यर्थेषु चिन्ता तदतिपरतया भ्राम्यमाणस्य नित्यम्।
तावन्नार्थस्य सिद्धिर्भवति कथमपि प्रार्थितस्यर्तिभाजा
कैवल्याख्यस्य लोके रमणसुखभुवो मुक्तदोषानुषक्तेः॥२७॥

निष्कामा मुनयः परावरदृशो निर्धूतपाप्मोदया
निस्संगा निरहंकृता निरुपमानन्दं परं लेभिरे।
यद्गत्वा न लुठन्ति मातृजठरे दुःखाकरे मानवा
दुर्गन्धे पुनरेत्य काममकरे संसारपाथोनिधौ॥२८॥

ब्रह्मामृतं भज सदा सहजप्रकाशं
सर्वान्तरं निरवधि प्रथितप्रभावम्।
यद्यस्ति ते जिगमिषा सहसा भवाब्धेः
पारे परे परमशर्मणि निष्कलंके॥२९॥

चिदेव ध्यातव्या सततमनवद्या सुखतनु-
र्निराधारा नित्या निरवधिरविद्यादिरहिता।
अनास्थामास्थाय भ्रमवपुषि सर्वत्र विषये
सदाशेषव्याख्यानिपुणमतिभिः ख्यातयतिभिः॥३०॥

यत्साक्षादभिधातुमक्षमतया शब्दाद्यनालिङ्गितं
कूटस्थं प्रतिवादयन्ति विलयद्वारा प्रपञ्चस्त्रजः।
मोक्षाय श्रुतयो निरस्तविधयोऽज्ञानस्य चोच्छित्तये
तत्राद्वैतवने सदा विचरताच्चेतः कुरङ्गः सताम्॥३१॥

तुल्यार्थेन त्वमैक्यं त्रिभुवनजनकस्तत्पदार्थः प्रपद्य
प्रत्यक्षं मोहजन्म त्यजति भगवति त्वंपदार्थोऽपि जीवः।
श्रुत्याचार्यप्रसादान्निरुपमविलसद्ब्रह्मविद्यस्तदैक्यं
प्राप्यानन्दप्रतिष्ठो भवति विगलितानाद्यविद्यो निरीहः॥३२॥

अहं ब्रह्मास्मीति स्फुरदमलबोधो यदि भवे-
त्पुमान् पुण्योद्रेकादुपचितपरानर्थविरतिः।
तदानीं क्वाविद्या क्व च तव ममेत्यल्पविषयो-
ऽभिमानः संसारः क्व च विविधदुःखैकवसतिः॥३३॥

हित्वा विश्वाद्यवस्थाः प्रकृतिविलसिता जाग्रदाद्यैर्विशेषैः
सार्धं चैतन्यधातौ प्रकृतिमपि समं कार्यजातैरशेषैः।
ज्ञानानन्दं तुरीयं विगलितगुणकं देशकालाद्यतीतं
स्वात्मानं वीतनिद्रः सततमधिकृतश्चिन्तयेदद्वितीयम्॥३४॥

संन्यासो विहितस्य केशवपदद्वन्द्वे व्यधायि श्रुता
वेदान्ता निरवद्यनिष्कलपरानन्दा सुनिष्ठाश्चिरम्।
संसारे वधबन्धदुःखबहुले मायाविलासेऽव्ययं
ब्रह्मास्मीति विहाय नान्यदधुना कर्तव्यमास्ते क्वचित्॥३५॥

अग्रे पश्चादधस्तादुपरि च परितो दिक्षु चान्यास्वनादि
कूटस्था संविदेका सकलतनुभृतामन्तरात्मानियन्त्री।
यस्यानन्दस्वभावा स्फुरति शुभधियः प्रत्यहं निष्प्रपञ्चा
जीवन्मुक्तः स लोके जयति गतमहामोहविश्वप्रपञ्चः॥३६॥

ते धन्या भुवने सुशिक्षितपरब्रह्मात्मविद्या जना
लोकानामनुरंजका हरिकथापीयूषपानप्रियाः।
येषां नाकतरंगिणीतटशिलाबद्धासनानां सतां
प्राणा यान्ति लयं सुखेन मनसा श्रीरंगचिन्ताभृताम्॥३७॥

शिव शिव महाभ्रान्तिस्थानं सतां विदुषामपि
प्रकृतिचपला धात्रा सृष्टाः स्त्रियो हरिणीदृशः।
विजहति धनं प्राणैः साकं यतस्तदवाप्त्ये
जगति मनुजा रागकृष्टास्तेदेकपरायणाः॥३८॥

हरति वपुषः कान्तिं पुंसः करोति बलक्षतिं
जनयति भृशं भ्रान्तिं नारी सुखाय निषेविता।
विरतिविरसा भुक्ता यस्मात्ततो न विवेकिभि-
र्विषयविमुखैः सेव्या मायासमाश्रितविग्रहा॥३९॥

कमलवदना पीनोत्तुङ्गं घटाकृति बिभ्रती
स्तनयुगमियं तन्वी श्यामा विशालंगचला।
विशददशना मध्ये क्षामा वृथेति जनाः श्रमं
विदधति मुधा रागादुच्चैरनीदृशवर्णने॥४०॥

यद्येता मदनेषवो मृगदृशश्चेतः कुरङ्गारयो
धीराणामपि नो भवेयुरबलाः संसारमायापुरे।
को नामामृतसागरे न रमते धीरस्तदा निर्मले
पूर्णानन्दमहोर्मिरम्यनिकरे रागादिनक्रोज्झिते॥४१॥

बालेयं बालभावं त्यजति न सुदती यत्कटाक्षैर्विशालै-
रस्मान्विभ्रामयन्ती लसदधरदलक्षिप्तचूतप्रवाला।
नेतुं वाञ्छत्यकामान् स्वसदनमधुना क्रीडितुं दत्तचित्तान्
पुष्यन्नीलोत्पलाभे मुरजिति कमलोवल्लभे गोपलीले॥४२॥

जनयति सुतं कश्चिन्नारी सती कुलभूषणं
निरुपमगुणैः पुण्यात्मानं जगत्परिपालनम्।
कथमपि न सा निन्द्या वन्द्या भवेन्महतां यतः
सुरसरिदिव ख्याता लोके पवित्रितभूतला॥४३॥

किं स्थानस्य निरीक्षणेन मुरजिद्ध्यानाय भूमण्डले
भ्रातश्चेद्विरतिर्भवेद्दृढतरा स्त्रक्चन्दनादौ सदा।
सा चैषा यदि नास्ति हन्त सुतरां व्यर्थं तदन्वेषणं
स्थानस्यानधिकारिणः सुरधुनीतीराद्रिकुञ्जादिषु॥४४॥

जानन्नेव करोति कर्म बहुलं दुःखात्मकं प्रेरितः
केनाप्यप्रतिवाच्यशक्तिमहिमा देवेन मुक्तात्मना।
सर्वज्ञेन हृदि स्थितेन मनुजः संसाररङ्गाङ्गणे
माद्यद्बुद्धिनटीविनोदनिपुणो नृत्यन्ननप्रियः॥४५॥

कर्तव्यं न करोति बन्धुभिरपि स्नेहात्मभिर्बोधितः
कामित्वादवमन्यते निजहितं धीरोप्यभीष्टं नरः।
निष्कामस्य न विक्रिया तनुभृतो लोके क्वचिदृश्यते
यत्तस्मादिदमेव मूलमखिलानर्थस्य निर्धारितम्॥४६॥

यदा देवादीनामपि भवति जन्मादि नियतं
महारम्ये स्थाने ललितललनालोलमनसाम्।
तदा कामार्तानां सुगतिरिह संसारजलधौ
निमग्नानामुच्चैरतिविषयशोकादिमकरे॥४७॥

न जानीषे चेतः क्वचिदपि हितं लोकमहितं
भ्रमद्भोगाकांक्षाकलुषिततया मोहबहुले।
जगत्यत्रारण्ये प्रतिपदमनेकापदि सदा
हरिध्याने व्यग्रं भव सकलतापैककदने॥४८॥

सद्वंशो गुणवानहं सुचरितः श्लाघां करोत्यात्मनो
नीचानां विदधाति च प्रतिदिनं सेवां जनानां द्विजः।
यो वित्तस्य जिघृक्षया स च कुतो नो लज्जते सज्जना-
लोल्भान्धस्य नरस्य नो खलु सतां दृष्ट हि लज्जाभयम्॥४९॥

नान्नं जीर्यति किंचिदौषधबलं नालं स्वकार्योदये
शक्तिश्चक्रमणे न हन्त जरया जीर्णीकृतायां तनौ।
अस्माकं त्वधुना न लोचनबलं पुत्रेति चिन्ताकुलो
ग्लायन्यर्थपरायणोऽतिकृपणो मिथ्याभिमानी गृही॥५०॥

अद्य श्वो वा मरणमशिवं प्राणिनां कालपाशै-
राकृष्टानां जगति भवति नान्यधात्वं कदाचित्।
यद्यप्येवं न खलु कुरुते हा तथाप्यर्थलोभं
हित्वा प्राणी हितमवहितो देवलोकानुकूलम्॥५१॥

रे रे वित्तमदान्धमोहबधिरा मिथ्याभिमानोद्धता
व्यर्थेयं भवतां धनावनरतिः संसारकारागृहे।
बद्धानां निगडेन गात्रममतासंज्ञेन यत्कर्हिचित्
देवब्राह्मणभिक्षुकादिषु धनं स्वप्नेऽपि न व्येति वः॥५२॥

नाभ्यस्तो धातुवादो न च युवतिवशी कारकः कोप्युपायो
नो वा पौराणिकत्वं न सरसकविता नापि नीतिर्न गीतिः।
तस्मादर्थार्थिनां या न भवति भवतश्चातुरीकापि विद्वन्
ज्ञात्वेत्थं चक्रपाणेरनुसर चरणाम्भोजयुग्मं विभूत्यै॥५३॥

अर्थेभ्योऽनर्थजातं भवति तनुभुतां यौवनादिष्ववश्यं
पित्राद्यैरर्जितेभ्योऽनुपकृतिमतिभिः स्वात्मना वर्जितेभ्यः।
यस्माद्दुःखाकरेभ्यस्तमनुसर सदा भद्र लक्ष्मीविलासं
गोपालं गोपकान्ताकुचकलशतटीकुंकुमासंगरंगम्॥५४॥

गाद्यत्तार्किकतान्त्रिकद्विपद्यटासंघट्टपंचानन-
स्तद्वद्दृप्तकृतान्तवैद्यककलाकल्पोऽपि निष्किञ्चनः।
यत्र क्वापि धनाशया कृशतनुर्भूपालसेवापरे
जीवन्नेव मृतायते किमपरं संसारदुःसागरे॥५५॥

जगाम व्यर्थं मे बहुदिनमथार्थर्थि तनयाः
कुभूमिपालानां निकटमतिदोषाकुलमतेः।
हरिध्यानव्यग्रं भवितुमधुना वाञ्छति मनः
क्वचिद्वगङ्गातीरे तरुणतुलसीसौरभभरे॥५६॥

अन्नाशाय सदा रटन्ति पृथकाः क्षुत्क्षामकण्ठा स्त्रियो
वासोभी रहिता बहिर्यवहृतौ निर्यान्ति नो लज्ज्या।
गेहादंगणमार्जनेऽपि गृहिणो यस्येति दुर्जीतं
यद्यप्यस्ति तथापि तस्य विरतिर्नोदेति चित्रं गृहे॥५७॥

हिक्काकासभगन्दरोदरमहामेदज्वरैराकुला
श्लेस्माद्यैरपि निद्रया विरहितो मन्दानलोऽल्पाशनः।
तारुण्येऽपि विलोक्यते बहुविधो जीवो दरिद्रेश्वरो
हा कष्टं कथमीदृशं भगवतः संसारदुःसागरे॥५८॥

आरभ्य गर्भवसतिं मरणावसानं
यद्यस्ति जीवितुमदृष्टमनेककालम्।
जन्तोस्तथापि न सुखं सुखविभ्रमोऽयं
यद्बालया रतिरनेकविभूतिभाजः॥५९॥

सन्त्यर्था मन सञ्चिताश्च बहुधाः पित्रादिभिः साम्प्रतं
वाणिज्यैः कृषिभिः कलाभिरपि तान्विस्तारयिष्यामि वः।
हे पुत्रा इति भावयन्ननुदिनं संसारपाशावलिं
छेत्तायं नु कथं मनोरथमयी जीवो निरालम्बनः॥६०॥

माता मृता जनयितापि जगाम शीघ्रं
लोकान्तरं तव कलत्रसुतादयोऽपि।
भ्रातस्तथापि न जहासि मृषाभिमानं
दुःखात्मके वपुषि मूत्रकुदर्पकूपे॥६१॥

कामव्याघ्रे कुमतिफणिनि स्वान्तदुर्वारनीडे
मायासिंहीविहरणवने लोभभल्लूकभीमे।
जन्मन्यस्मिन् भवति विरतिः सज्जनानां कदाचि-
त्तत्त्वज्ञानां विषयविषमाकण्टकाकीर्णपार्श्वे॥६२॥

स्वाधीने निकटस्थितेऽपि विमलज्ञानामृते मानसे
विख्याते मुनिसेवितेऽपि कुधियो न स्नान्ति तीर्थे द्विजाः।
यत्तत्कष्टमहो विवेकरहितास्तीर्थार्थिनो दुःखिता
यत्र काप्यख्वीमटन्ति जलधौ मज्जन्ति दुःखाकरे॥६३॥

त्वत्साक्षिकं सकलमेतदवोचमिथ्यं
भ्रातर्विचार्य भवता करणीयमिष्टम्।
येनेदृशं न भवति भवतोऽपि कष्टं
शोकाकुलस्य भवसागरमग्नमूर्तेः॥६४॥

यत्प्रीत्यर्थमनेकधाऽलभि मया कष्टेन वस्तु प्रियं
स्वस्याशाकवलीकृतेन विकलीभावं दधानेन मे।
तत्सर्वं विलयं निनाय भगवान् यो लीलया निर्जरे
मां हित्वा जरयाकुलीकुततनुं कालाय तस्मै नमः॥६५॥

आयुर्वेदविदां रसाशनवतां पथ्याशिनां यत्नतो
वैद्यानामपि रोगजन्म वपुषो ह्यन्तर्यतो दृश्यते।
दुश्चक्षुःकवलीकृतत्रिभुवनो लीलाविहारस्थितः
सर्वोपायविनाशनैकचतुरः कालाय तस्मै नमः॥६६॥

दष्टं प्रायो विकलमखिलं कालसर्पेण विश्वं
क्रूरेणेदं शिवशिव मुने ब्रूहि रक्षाप्रकारम्।
अस्यास्त्येकं शृणु मुररिपोर्ध्यानिपीयूषपानं
त्यक्त्वा नान्यत्किमपि भुवने दृश्यते शास्त्रदृष्ट्या॥६७॥

कश्चित्क्रन्दति कालकर्कशकराकृष्टं विनष्टं हठा-
दुत्कृष्टं तनयं विलोक्य पुरतः पुत्रेति हा हा क्वचित्।
कश्चिन्नर्तकनर्तकीपरिवृतो नृत्यतीह कुत्रचि-
च्चित्रं संसृतिपद्धतिः प्रथयति प्रीतिश्च कष्टश्च नः॥६८॥

सा रोगिणी यदि भवेदथवा विवर्णा
बालप्रिया शशिमुखी रसिकस्य पुंसः।
शल्यायते हृदि तथामरणं कृशांगी
यत्तस्य सा विगतनिद्रसरोरुहाक्षी॥६९॥

निष्कंटकेऽपि न सुखं वसुधाधिपत्ये
कस्यापि राजतिलकस्य यदेष देवः।
विश्वेश्वरो भुजगराजविभूतिभूषो
हित्वा तपस्यति चिरं सकला विभूतिः॥७०॥

कदाचित्कष्टेन द्रविणमधमाराधनवशा-
न्मया लब्धं स्तोकं निहितमवनौ तस्करभयात्।
ततो नैजे कश्चित्क्वचिदपि तदाखुर्बिलगृहे
न यल्लब्धोऽप्यर्थो न भवति यदा कर्म विषमम्॥७१॥

स्वयं भोक्ता दाता वसु सुबहु संपाद्य भविता
कुटुम्बानां पोष्टा गुणनिधिरशेषेप्सितनरः।
इति प्रत्याशस्य प्रबलादुरितानीतविधुरं
शिरस्यस्याकस्मात्पतति निधनं येन भवति॥७२॥

भानुर्भूवलयप्रदक्षिणठातिः क्रीडारतिः सर्वदा
चन्द्रोऽप्येष कलानिधिः कवलितः स्वर्भानुना दुःखितः।
ह्रासं गच्छति वर्धते च सततं वीर्वाणविश्रामभू-
स्तत्स्थानं खलु यत्र नास्त्यपहतिः क्लेशस्य संसारिणाम्॥७३॥

भूमण्डलं लयमुपैति भवत्यबाधं
लब्धात्मकं पुनरपि प्रलयं प्रयाति।
आवर्तते सकलमेतदंनन्तवारं
ब्रह्मादिभिः सममहो न सुखं जनानाम्॥७४॥

अहांऽत्यर्थेऽप्यर्थे श्रुतिशतगुरुभ्यामवगते
निषिद्धत्वेनापि प्रतिदिवसमाधावति मनः।
पिशाचस्तत्रैव स्थिररतिरसारेऽपि चपलो
न जाने केनास्य प्रतिकृतिरनार्यस्य भविता॥७५॥

अरे चेतिश्चित्रं भ्रमसि यदपास्य प्रियतमं
मुकुन्दं पार्श्वस्थं पितरमपि मान्यं सुमनसाम्।
बहिःशब्दाधर्थे प्रकृतिचपले क्लेशबहुले
न ते संसारेऽस्मिन्भवति सुखदाद्यापि विरतिः॥७६॥

अहं श्रान्तोऽध्वानं बहुविधमतिक्रम्य विषमं
धनाकांक्षाक्षिप्तः कुनृपतिमुखालोकनपरः।
इदानीं केनापि स्थितिमुदरकूपस्य भरणे
कदन्नेनारण्ये क्वचिदपि समीहे स्थिरमतिः॥७७॥

सा गोष्ठी सुहृदां निवारितसुधास्वादाधुना क्वागम-
त्ते धीरा धरणीधरोपकरणीभूता ययुः क्वापरे।
ते भूपा भवभीरवो भवरताः क्वागुर्निरस्तारयो
हा कष्टं क्व च गम्यते न हि सुखं काप्यस्ति लोकत्रये॥७८॥

उदासीनो देवो मदनमथनः सज्जनकुले
कतिक्रीडासक्तः कृतपरिजनः प्राकृतजनः।
इयं म्लेच्छाक्रान्ता त्रिदशतटिनी चोभयतटे
कथं भ्रातः स्थाता कथय सुकृतिन कुत्र विभयः॥७९॥

निस्सारा वसुधाऽधुना समजनि पौढप्रतापानल-
ज्वालाजालसमाकुला द्विपघटासंघट्टविक्षोभिता।
म्लेच्छानां रथवाजिपत्तिनिवहैरुन्मूलिता कीदृशी
यं विद्या भवितेति हन्त न सखे जानीमहे मोहिताः॥८०॥

वेदो निर्वेदमागादिह नमनभिया ब्राह्मणानां वियोगा-
द्वेयासिक्यो गिरोऽपि क्वचिदपि विरलाः साम्प्रतं सन्ति देशे।
इत्थं धर्मे विलीने यवनकुलपतौ शासति क्षोणिबिंबं
नित्यं गंगावगाहद्भवति गतिरितः संसृतेरर्थसिद्धौ॥८१॥

गंगा गंगेति यस्याः श्रुतमपि पठितं केनचिन्नाममात्रं
दूरस्थस्यापि पुंसो दलयति दुरितं प्रौढमित्याहुरेके।
सा गंगा कस्य सेव्या न भवति भुवने सज्जनस्याति भव्या
ब्रह्माण्डं प्लावयन्ती त्रिपुरहरजटामण्डलं मण्डयन्ती॥८२॥

कलौ गंगा काश्यां त्रिपुरहरपुर्यां भगवती
प्रशस्ता देवानामपि भवति सेव्याऽनुदिवसम्।
इति व्यासो ब्रूते मुनिजनधुरीणो हरिकथा-
सुधापानस्वस्थो गलितभवबंधोऽतुलमतिः॥८३॥

यस्याः संगतिरुन्नतिं वितनुते वाराममीषां जनै-
रुद्गीता कविभिर्महेश्वरमनोभीष्टा महीमण्डले।
सा सन्तः शरदिन्दुसोदरपयः पूराभिरामा नद-
त्कोकश्रेणिमनोज्ञपुण्यपुलिना भागीरथी सेव्यताम्॥८४॥

कदा भागीरथ्या भवजलधिसंसारतरणेः
स्खलद्वीचीमालाचपलतलविस्तारितमुदः।
तमःस्थाने कुञ्जे क्वचिदपि निविश्याहृतमना
भविष्याम्येकाकी नरकमथने ध्यानरसिकः॥८५॥

कदा गोविन्देति प्रतिदिवसमुल्लासमिलितः
सुधाधाराप्रायास्त्रिदशतहिनीवीचिमुखरे।
भविष्यन्त्येकान्ते क्वचिदपि निकुञ्जे मम गिरो
मरालीचक्राणां श्रुतिसुखरवाक्रान्तपुलिने॥८६॥

भजत विबुध साधवो लोकबन्धुं
हरहसिततरंगं शंकराशीर्षसंगम्।
दलितभवभुजङ्गं ख्यातमायाविभंगं
निखिलभुवनवन्धं सर्वतीर्थानवद्यम्॥८७॥

यममृतममृतानां भंगरंगप्रसंग-
प्रकटितरसवत्तावैभवं पीतमुच्चैः।
दलयति कलिदोषांस्तां सुपर्वस्रवन्तीं
किमिति न भजतार्ता ब्रह्मलोकावतीर्णाम्॥८८॥

यत्तीरे वसतां सतामपि जलैर्मूलैः फलैर्जीवतां
मुक्ताहंममभावशुद्धमनसामाचारविद्यावताम्।
केवल्यं करबिल्वतुल्यममलं संपद्यते हेलया
सा गंगा ह्यतुलामलोर्मिपटला सद्भिः कुतो नेक्ष्यते॥८९॥

तीर्थानामवलोकने सुमनसामुत्कण्ठते मानसं
तावद्भवलये सतां पुररिपुध्यानामृतास्वादिनाम्।
यावत्ते न विलोकयन्ति सरितां रोचिष्णुमुक्तावलीं
श्रीमन्नाकतरंगिणीं हरजटाजूटाटवीविभ्रमाम्॥९०॥

संसारो विविधाधिबाधविधुरः सारायते मानसे
निस्सारोपि वपुष्मतां कलिवृकग्रासीकृतानां चिरम्।
इष्टायां घनसारपार्थास महापुण्येन यस्यां सतां
सा सेव्या न कुतो भवेत्सुरधुनी स्वर्गापवर्गोदया॥९१॥

नदन्ती चेतो नो क्वचिद्धंसश्रेणी सुखयति रिरंसुः श्रुतिसुखं
विपुलपुलिने मंथरगतिः।
हरन्ती पापौघान् सुरतरुवृता नाकतटिनी
सदा सद्भिः सेव्या सकलपुरुषार्थाय कृतिभिः॥९२॥

यामासाद्य त्रिलोकीजनमहितशिवावल्लभारामभूमिं
ब्रह्मदीनां सुराणां सुखवसतिभुवां मण्डलं मण्डयन्ति।
नो गर्भे व्यालुठन्ति क्वचिदपि मनुजा मातुरुत्क्रान्तिभाज
स्तां काशीं नो भजन्ते किमिति सुमतयो दुःखभारं वहन्तः॥९३॥

विद्यन्ते द्वारकाद्या जगति बहुविधा देवताराजधान्यो
यद्यप्यन्यास्तथापि स्वलदमलजलावर्तगंगातरंगा।
काश्येवारामकूजत्पिकशुकचटकाक्रान्तदिक्कामिनीनां
क्रीडाकासारशाला जयति मुनिजनानन्दकन्दैकभूमिः॥९४॥

काशीयं समलंकृता निरुपमस्वर्गापगासंभव-
स्थूलोत्तारतरंग बिन्दुविलसन्मुक्ताफलश्रेणिभिः।
चञ्चच्चञ्चलचञ्चरीकनिकरश्यामाम्बरा राजते
कारारस्थविनिद्रपद्मनयना विश्वेश्वरप्रेयसी॥९५॥

वह्निप्राकारबुद्धिं जनयति वलभीवासिनां नागराणां
गन्धारण्यप्रसूतस्फुटकुसुमचयः किंशुकानां शुकानाम्।
चञ्चाकारो वसन्ते परमपदपदं राजधानी पुरारेः
सा काश्यारामरम्या जयति मुनिजनानन्दकन्दैकभूमिः॥९६॥

किं कुर्मः कं भजामः किमिह समुदितं साधनं भो वयस्याः
संसारोन्मूलनाय प्रतिदिवसमिहानर्थशंकावतारः।
भ्रातर्ज्ञातं निदानं भवभयदलने संगतं सज्जनानां
तां काशीमाश्रयामो निरपमयशसः स्वःस्रवन्त्या वयस्याम्॥९७॥

मुक्तिः क्वापि न मुक्तिरस्त्यभिमता क्वाप्यस्ति मुक्तिर्न सा
काश्यामस्ति विशेष एव सुतरां श्लाघ्यं यदेतद्द्वयम्।
सर्वैरुत्तममध्यमाधमजनैरासाधतेऽनुग्रहा-
देवस्य त्रिपुरद्विषः सुरधुनीस्नानावदातव्ययैः॥९८॥

सन्त्यन्ये त्रिदशापगादिपतनात्पुण्याः प्रयागादयः
प्रालेयाचलसंभवा बहुफलाः सिद्धाश्रमाः सिद्धयः।
यत्राघौघदहा भवन्ति सुधियां ध्यानेश्वराणां चिरं
मुक्ताशेषभियां विनिद्रमनसां कन्दाम्बुपर्णाशिनाम्॥९९॥

केदारस्थानमेकं रुचिरतमुमानाय्यलीलावनीकं
प्रालेयाद्रिप्रदेशे प्रथितभतितरामस्ति गंगानिवेशे।
ख्यातं नारायणस्य त्रिजगति बदरीनाम सिद्धाश्रमस्य
तत्रैवानादिमूर्तेर्मुनिजनमनसामन्यदानन्दमूर्तेः॥१००॥

॥इति श्रीमद्राजर्षिप्रवरभर्तृहरिकृतं विज्ञानशतकं संपूर्णम्॥

ALPHABETICAL INDEX OF VERSES

अकरुणत्वमकारण-	12
अच्छाच्छ चन्दनरसा-	52
अज्ञः सुखमाराध्यः	1
अपसर सखे दूरा-	43
अवश्यं यातारश्चिर-	60
अर्धं सुप्त्वा निशायाः	55
अजानन्माहात्म्यं	62
अधिगतपरमार्थान्	4
असाराः सन्त्वेते	39
असूचीसंचारे	54
अग्राह्यं हृदयं	98
अनावर्ती कालो	90
अकिञ्चनस्य दान्तस्य	104
अतिक्रान्तः कालो	95
अभिमतमहामान	63
अभिमुखनिहतस्य	98
अप्रियवचनदरिद्रैः	96
अमीषां प्राणानां	58
अभुक्तायां यस्यां	75
अग्रे गीतं सरसकवयः	77
अम्भोजिनीवननिवास-	5
आवासः किल	51
आमीलितनयनानां	36
आसारेण न हर्म्यति	55
आरम्भगुर्वी क्षयिणी	14
आसंसारं त्रिभुवनमिदं	82
आवासः क्रियतां गाङ्गे	40
आज्ञा कीर्तिः पालनं	11
अर्थानामीशिषे त्वं	73
आयुर्वर्षशतं नृणां	72
आदित्यस्य गतागतै-	70
आयुः कल्लोललोलं	68
आधिव्याधिशतै-	67
आक्रान्तं मरणेन	66
आवर्तः संशयानां	41
आशीमहि वयं भिक्षा	74
आशा नाम नदी	60
अहो धन्याः केचित्त्रुटित-	95
इयत्येतस्मिन्वा निरवधि-	98
इमे तारुण्यश्रीनवपरिमलाः	34
इतो विद्युद्वल्ली	54
इयं बाला मां	46
इह हि मधुरगीतं	44
इदमनुचितमक्रमश्च	36
इतः स्वपिति केशवः	19
उद्यानेषु विचित्र	89
उत्तिष्ठ क्षणमेकमुद्वह	90
उद्वृत्तः स्तनभार एव	33

उदन्वच्छन्ना भूः 97
उरसि निपतितानां 36
उन्मत्तप्रेमसंरम्भा– 49
उन्मीलस्तिरंग 42
उपरि धनं धनपटलं 53
उद्भासिताखिलखलस्य 14
उत्खातं निधिशङ्कया 58
एकाकी निस्पृहः 84
एतां हसन्ति च रुदन्ति 90
एताश्चलद्वलयसंहति- 31
एको देवः केशवो वा 97
एकेनापि हि शूरेण 104
ऐश्वर्यस्य विभूषणं 22
एते सत्पुरुषाः परार्थ- 18
एतस्माद्विरमेन्द्रियार्थ- 76
कश्चुम्बति कुलपुरुषो 45
कदर्थितस्यापि हि 22
कदा वारणस्या– 83
कमठकुलाचल 97
करे श्लाघ्यस्त्यागः 15
क्वचिद्वीणावादः 91
कृच्छ्रेणामेध्यमध्ये 68
कृमिकुलचितं 3
कृश काणः खञ्जः 50
क्वचित्सभ्रुभङ्गैः 30
क्वचिद्भूमीशायी 21
कान्ताकटाक्षविशिखा 21
कार्कश्यं स्तनयोदृशो- 90
कार्यायत्तं फलं पुंसां 103
कान्तेत्युत्पललोचनेति 40
कामिनीकायकान्तारे 44
किमिह बहुभीरुक्तैः- 40
किं कन्दाः कन्दरेभ्यः 64
किं गतेन यदि सा 47
किं तेन हेमगिरिणा 88
किं वेदैः स्मृतिभिः 78
कुङ्कुमपङ्ककलङ्कितदेहा 31
कुसुमस्तबकस्यैव 8
केशानाकुलयन् दृशो 56
केशाः संयमिनः 32
केयूरा न विभूषयन्ति 5
को न याति वशं 101
को लाभो गुणिसंगमः 103
कौपीनं शतखण्डजर्जरतरं 84
क्षणं बालो भूत्वा 72
क्षान्तं न क्षमया 58
क्षान्तिश्चेत्कवचेन किं 5
क्षुद्राः सन्ति सहस्रशः 102
क्षीरेणात्मगतोदकाय 18
क्षुत्क्षामोऽपि जराकृशोऽपि 7
खलोल्लापाः सोढाः 58
खल्वाटो दिवसेश्वरस्य 23
गजभुजंग 22
गङ्गातरङ्गहिमशीकर- 64
गङ्गातीरे हिमगिरिशिला 87
गात्रं संकुचितं गति- 79
गात्रैर्गिरा च विकल- 61
गुणवदगुणवद्वा कुर्वता 26

गुरुणा स्तनभारेण	33	मोहं मार्जय तामुपार्जय	76
चला लक्ष्मीश्चला:	91	पद्माकरं दिनकरो	18
चाण्डाल: किमयं	86	परिचरितव्या: सन्तो	88
चूडोत्तंसितचारुचन्द्र	57	परिमलभृतो वाता:	51
चुम्बन्तो गण्डभित्ती-	56	परिवर्तिनि संसारे	7
चेतश्चिन्तय मा रमां	77	परिक्षीण: कश्चित्स्पृहयति	10
जयन्ति ते सुकृतिनो	6	परिभ्रमसि किं वृथा	76
जल्पन्ति सार्धमन्येन	43	पत्रं नैव यदा करीर-	96
जीर्णा एव मनोरथा:	82	पापान्निवारयति योजयते	18
जीर्णा कन्था: तत:	96	पाणि: पात्रं पवित्रं	87
जात्यन्धाय च दुर्मुखाय	45	पातालमाविशसि यासि	78
जातिर्यातु रसातलं	9	पान्थस्त्रीविरहानला-	52
जात: कूर्म: स एक:	19	पुण्ये ग्रामे वने वा	63
जाड्यं धियो हरति	6	पुरा विद्वत्तासीदुपशमवतां	94
जाड्यं ह्रीमति गण्यते	12	परेषां चेतांसि प्रतिदिवस-	75
तपस्यन्त: सन्त: किमधि-	80	पुण्यैर्मूलफलै:	64
तरुणी वेषोद्दीपितकामा	53	प्रणयमधुरा: प्रेमद्वारा	34
तस्मादनन्तमजरं परमं	78	प्रदानं प्रच्छन्नं	16
तस्या: स्तनौ यदि घनौ	34	प्रशान्तशास्त्रार्थविचार-	92
तावदेव कृतिनामपि	48	प्रसह्य मणिमुद्धरेन्मकर-	1
तावन्महत्त्वं पाण्डित्यं	49	प्रथित: प्रणयवतीनां	52
तुङ्गं वेश्म सुता: सता-	62	प्राङ्मामेति मनागना-	35
तृषा शुष्यत्यास्ये पिबति	62	प्राप्ता: श्रिय: सकल-	77
तृष्णां छिन्धि भज क्षमां	19	प्राय: कन्दुकपातेनोत्	23
तानीन्द्रियाणि सकलानि	100	प्राणाघातान्निवृत्ति:	15
त्वमेव चातकाधारोऽसीति	101	प्रारभ्यते न खलु	20
त्वं राजा वयमप्यु-	73	प्रियसखि विपदण्डा-	24
मृत्पिण्डो जलरेखया	73	प्रिया न्याया वृत्तिर्मलिन-	16
मुखेन चन्द्रकान्तेन	33	प्रोद्यत्प्रौढप्रियङ्गु-	56

फलमलमशनाय 74
फलं स्वेच्छालभ्यं 65
ब्रह्मज्ञानविवेकनिर्मल- 61
ब्रह्माण्डमण्डलीमात्रं 85
ब्रह्मा येन कुलालव- 25
ब्रह्मेन्द्रादिमरुद्गणा 9
बाले लीलामुकुलितमयी 46
बोद्धारो मत्सरग्रस्ताः 1
भक्तिर्भवे मरणजन्मभयं 78
भग्नाशस्य करण्डपीडित- 23
भवन्ति नम्रास्तरवः 17
भव्यं भक्तं ततः किं 92
भ्रान्तं देशमनेकदुर्गविषमं 57
भिक्षा कामदुघा धेनुः 88
भिक्षाशी जनमध्यसंगरहितः 86
भिक्षासनं तदपि नीरस- 61
भिक्षाहारमदैन्यमप्रति- 66
भीमं वनं भवति 28
भूः पर्यङ्को निजभुजलता 93
भ्रूचातुर्यात् कुञ्चिताक्षाः 29
भोगा न भुक्ता 59
भोगा भङ्गुरवृत्तयो 69
भोगा मेघवितानमध्य- 67
भोगास्तुङ्गतरङ्गभङ्ग- 67
भोगे रोगभयं कुले 66
मज्जत्वम्भसि यातु 27
मुग्धे धानुष्कता 32
मत्तेभकुम्भदलने 49
मधु तिष्ठति वाचि 43
मधुरयं मधुरैरपि 51
मणिः शाणोल्लीढः 10
मनसि वचसि काये 20
महादेवो देवः सरिदपि 95
मही रम्या शय्या 85
महेश्वरे वा जगतामधीश्वरे 83
मातर्मेदिनि तात मारुत 87
मातर्लक्ष्मि भजस्व 85
ददतु ददतु गाली- 91
दानं भोगो नाश- 10
दाक्षिण्यं स्वजने 6
दिक्कालाद्यनवच्छिन्ना- 1
दिश वनहरिणेभ्यो 38
दीना दीनमुखैः 63
दुर्जनः परिहर्तव्यो 12
दूरादर्थं घटयति 102
दूराराध्याश्चामी 80
द्रष्टव्येषु किमुत्तमं 31
दैवेन प्रभुणा स्वयं 25
दौर्मन्त्र्यान्नृपतिः 10
धन्यानां गिरिकन्दरे 61
धन्यास्त एव धवला- 45
न कश्चिच्चण्डकोपाना- 13
नगभ्यो मन्त्राणां 44
न ध्यातं पदमीश्वरस्य 71
न नटा न विटा 74
न संसारोत्पन्नं चरितमनु- 60
न भिक्षा दुष्प्रापा पथि 92
नमस्यामो देवान्ननु 25

नम्रत्वेनोन्नमन्तः परगुण- 17
नामृतं न विषं 41
नायं ते समयो 89
निन्दन्तु नीतिनिपुणाः 21
निवृत्ता भोगेच्छा 60
नूनमाज्ञाकरस्तस्याः 32
नूनं हि ते कविवराः 32
नेता यस्य बृहस्पतिः 23
नैवाकृतिः फलति नैव 27
नो खड्गप्रविदारिताः 92
नो सत्येन मृगाङ्क 41
नाभ्यस्ता भुवि वादि- 71
मालतीकुसुमस्यैव द्वे 97
मालती शिरसि जृम्भ- 35
माने म्लायति खण्डिते 81
मात्सर्यमुत्सार्य विचार्य 39
मृगमीनसज्जनानां 14
यत्रानेके क्वचिदपि गृहे 70
यद्धात्रा निजभालपट्टलिखितं 11
यद्वक्त्रं मुहुरीक्षसे न 93
यदचेतनोऽपि पादैः 9
यदा किंचिज्ज्ञोऽहं द्विप इव 3
यन्नागा मदवारिभिन्न- 102
यदा मेरुः श्रीमान्निपतति 79
यदा योगाभ्यासव्यसनकृश- 47, 103
यदेतत्पूर्णेन्दुद्युतिहरमुदार- 42
यदेतत्स्वच्छन्दं विहरण- 82
यस्यास्ति वित्तं स नरः 9
यावत्स्वस्थमिदं शरीरमरुजं 80
या साधुंश्च खलान्करोति 26
येनैवाम्बरखण्डेन 24
ये वर्धन्ते धनपतिपुरः 65
येषां न विद्या न तपो 102
ये सन्तोषनिरन्तरप्रमुदिता 65
यूयं वयं वयं यूयमित्य- 96
यः प्रीणयेत् 18
रक्तत्वं कमलानां 102
रम्यं हर्म्यतलं न किं 81
रम्याश्चन्द्रमरीचयस्तृणवती 81
रत्नैर्महार्हैस्तुतुषुर्न देवा 20
रागास्यागारमेकं 37
राजन्दुधुक्षसि यदि 11
राजंस्तृष्णाम्बुराशेर्न हि 36
रात्रिः सैव पुनः स 70
रे कन्दर्प करं 46, 98
रे रे चातक सावधान- 101
लज्जागुणौघजननीं 21
लभेत सिकतासु 2
लाङ्गुलचालनमध- 7
लीलावतीनां सहजा 42
लोभश्चेदगुणेन किं 12
वक्त्रं चन्द्रविकासि 30
वचसि भवति सङ्ग- 48
वयं येभ्यो जाता- 12
वयमिह परितुष्टा 73
वर्णं सितं शिरसि 79
वलिभिर्मुखमाक्रान्तं 59
वहति भुवनश्रेणीं 8

वचो हि सत्यं	103	स्नात्वा गाङ्गैः पयोभिः	87
वरं तुङ्गाच्छृङ्गाद्गुरु-	24	स्थाल्यां वैदुर्यमय्यां	27
वरं पर्वतदुर्गेषु	99	सृजति तावदशेषगुणाकरं	24
वरं पक्षच्छेदः समदम-	8	संपत्सु महतां चित्तं	16
वह्निस्तस्य जलायते	22	संतप्तायसि संस्थितस्य	16
वाञ्छा सज्जनसंगमे	14	संसार तव पर्यन्त-	38
विद्या नाधिगता	72	स्वपरप्रतारकोऽसौ	48
विद्या नाम नरस्य	5	स्रजो हृद्यामोदा व्यजन-	53
विपदि धैर्यमथाभ्युदये	15	स्त्रीमुद्रां कुसुमायुधस्य	50
विपुलहृदयैर्धन्यैः	74	संसारे स्वप्नसारे	39
वियदुपचितमेघं	53	संसारेऽस्मिन्नसारे	37
विरमत बुधा योषित्	47	सिद्धाध्यासितकन्दरे	38
विरम विरसायासा-	25	स्मृता भवति तापाय	41
विरहेऽपि सङ्गमः	46	सत्यं जना वच्मि न	40
विश्रम्य विश्रम्य वने	34	साहित्यसङ्गीतकला-	100
विस्तारितं मकरकेतन-	43	संमोहयन्ति मदयन्ति	94
विश्वामित्रपराशरप्रभृ-	50	स्थितिः पुण्येरण्ये सह	99
वितीर्णे सर्वस्वे तरुण-	83	स्वादिष्टं मधुनो धृताच्च	99
वने रणे शत्रुजलाग्नि-	28	सिंहो बली द्विरद-	100
विवेकव्याकोशे विकसति	94	स्मितेन भावेन च	29
वेश्वासौ मदनज्वाला	45	स्मितं किञ्चिन्मुग्धं	30
व्याघ्रीव तिष्ठति जरा	68	स्वायत्तमेकान्तगुणं	2
व्यादीर्घेण चलेन	44	स्तनौ मांसग्रन्थी	62
व्यालं बालमृणालतन्तु-	2	सूनुः सच्चरितः सती	100
स जातः कोप्यासीन्मदन-	75	स्वल्पस्नायुवसावशेष-	7
सहकारकुसुमकेसर-	52	सन्त्यन्येऽपि बृहस्पति-	8
सति प्रदीपे सत्यग्नौ	33	सिंहः शिशुरपि	9
सत्यामेव त्रिलोकी-	89	सत्याऽनृता च परुषा	11
समारम्भाः भग्नाः	93	रम्या सा नगरी	69

शम्भुस्वयम्भुहरयो हरिणे-	29	शुधाशुभ्रं धाम स्फुरदमल-	53
शय्या शैलशिला गृहं	88	शुभ्रं सद्म सविभ्रमा	26
शशी दिवसधूसरो	13	श्रुङ्गारद्रुमनीरदे प्रसृम-	37
शशिदिवाकरयोर्ग्रहपीडनं	95	श्रोत्रं श्रुतेनैव न कुण्डलेन	17
शास्त्रज्ञोऽपि प्रगुणितनयो-	50	हर्तुर्याति न गोचरं	4
शास्त्रोपस्कृतशब्दसुन्दर-	4	हिंसाशून्यमयत्नलभ्यमशनं	86
शिरः शार्वं स्वर्गात्पशुपति-	3	हेमन्ते दधिदुग्धसर्पिरशना	55

Proverbial Expressions

ज्ञानलवदुर्विदग्धं ब्रह्मापि नरं न रञ्जयति।

विभूषणं मौनमपण्डितानाम्।

विवेकभ्रष्टानां भवति विनिपातः शतमुखः।

क्षीयन्ते खलु भूषणानि सततं वाग्भूषणं भूषणम्।

विद्या राजसु पूज्यते न तु धनं विद्याविहीनः पशुः।

सुकविता यद्यस्ति राज्येन किम्।

सत्संगतिः कथय किं न करोति पुंसाम्।

सर्वः कृच्छ्रगतोऽपि वाञ्छति जनः सत्त्वानुरूपं फलम्।

स जातो येन जातेन याति वंशः समुन्नतिम्।

महतां निःसीमानश्चरित्रविभूतयः।

न खलु वयस्तेजसो हेतुः।

सर्वे गुणाः काञ्चनमाश्रयन्ति।

नानाफलं फलति कल्पलतेव भूमिः।

वाराङ्गनेव नृपनीतिरनेकरूपा।

मणिना भूषितः सर्पः किमसौ न भयंकरः।

सेवाधर्मः परमगहनो येगिनामप्यगम्यः।

सन्तः स्वयं परहिते विहिताभियोगाः।

न निश्चितार्थाद्विरमन्ति धीराः।

मनस्वी कार्यार्थी गणयति न दुःखं न च सुखम्।

न्याय्यात्पथः प्रविचलन्ति पदं न धीराः।

शीलं परं भूषणम्।

दैवमेव हि परं वृद्धौ क्षये कारणम्।

प्रायेण साधुवृत्तानामस्थायिन्यो विपत्तयः।

स्पृशन्त्यास्तारुण्यं किमिव न हि रम्यं मृगदृशः।

पुण्यैर्विना न हि भवन्ति समीहितार्थाः।

तथाऽप्येतद्भूमौ न हि परहितात्पुण्यमधिकम्।

कन्दर्पदर्पदलने विरला मनुष्याः।

विपदि हन्त सुधापि विषायते।

सर्वं वस्तु भयान्वितं भुवि नृणां वैराग्यमेवाभयम्।

जीवे वारितरङ्गचञ्चलतरे सौख्यं कुतः प्राणिनाम्।

मनसि च परितुष्टे कोऽर्थवान्को दरिद्रः।

शरीरे का वार्ता करिकलभकर्णाग्रचपले।

संदीप्ते भवने तु कूपखननं प्रत्युद्यमः कीदृशः।

सुखं शान्तः शेते मुनिरतनुभूतिर्नृप इव।

नार्यः श्मशानघटिका इव वर्जनीयाः।

दारिद्र्यान्मरणं वरं वरमिति ज्ञात्वैव तूष्णीं स्थितः।

न जाने संसारः किममृतमयः किं विषमयः।

चलाचले च संसारे धर्म एको हि निश्चलः।

विधिरहो बलवानिति मे मतिः।

यत्पूर्वं विधिना ललाटलिखितं तन्मार्जितुं कः क्षमः।

नारी नाम विषाङ्कुरैरिव लता दोषैः समं वर्धिता।

शीलं हि सर्वस्य नरस्य भूषणम्।

सदा सन्तुष्टमनसः सर्वाः सुखमया दिशः।

Metres in the Śatakas

I

1. अनुष्टुप् I. 1, 2, 7, 20, 24, 25, 32, 42, 46, 49, 55, 62, 71, 77, 83, 87, 99
2. शालिनी I. 39.
3. द्रुतविलम्बित 41, 52, 85, 86.
4. वंशस्थ 61.
5. वसन्ततिलका 14, 19, 23, 37, 38, 48, 59, 63, 65, 72, 73, 79, 97, 100.
6. मालिनी 13, 70, 95.
7. पृथ्वी 4, 5, 45, 67.
8. मन्दाक्रान्ता 47.
9. शिखरिणी 8, 10, 28, 35, 36, 53, 56, 57, 74, 78, 91.
10. हरिणी 9, 27, 88, 89.
11. शार्दूलविक्रीडित 6, 11, 12, 15, 16, 17, 18, 21, 22, 26, 31, 33, 40, 43, 44, 51,, 58, 64, 66, 69, 79, 80, 81, 82, 84, 90, 92, 93, 94, 98.
12. स्रग्धरा I. 54, 60, 68, 96.
13. आर्या I. 3, 29, 30, 34, 50.

II

1. अनुष्टुप् 11, 13, 14, 16, 17, 33, 38, 42, 43, 44, 50, 54, 59, 75, 76.

2. इद्रवज्रा 40
3. उपजातिः 21, 36, 47.
4. शालिनी 3.
5. द्रुतविलम्बितः 82
6. वंशस्थः 2
7. वसन्ततिलका 1, 8, 10, 18, 53, 61, 73, 87
8. मालिनी 25, 34, 39, 56, 71, 91
9. मन्दाक्रान्ता 62, 77
10. शिखरिणी 4, 6, 19, 35, 48, 57, 63, 68, 69, 78, 88, 89, 93, 94
11. हरिणी 52, 67, 81
12. शार्दूलविक्रीडित 5, 7, 12, 15, 24, 30, 32, 41, 46, 49, 55, 58, 64, 79, 80, 83, 84, 95, 97, 100
13. स्रग्धरा 28, 29, 31, 37, 45, 74, 96, 98, 99
14. आर्या 26, 60, 65, 72, 85, 86, 92
15. दोधकम् 9
16. रथोद्धता 23, 66, 70
17. पुष्पिताग्रा 27
18. वियोगिनी 51
19. उपचित्रा 90

III

1. अनुष्टुप् 8, 55, 89, 92
2. उपजातिः 7
3. वंशस्थः 84
4. वसन्ततिलका 15, 24, 38, 67, 68, 69, 70, 74

5. मालिनी 53, 54
6. पृथ्वी 62
7. मन्दाक्रान्ता 28, 42, 66, 81, 98
8. वैतालीयम् 56
9. शिखरिणी 4, 5, 9, 11, 12, 16, 18, 19, 27, 48, 50, 58, 60, 61, 72, 76, 77, 82, 85, 86, 87, 94
10. हरिणी 22, 57
11. शार्दूलविक्रीडित 1, 2, 3, 6, 10, 13, 14, 17, 20, 21, 26, 29, 30, 31, 32, 33, 34, 35, 39, 40, 41, 43, 44, 45, 46, 47, 49, 50, 51, 59, 63, 64, 65, 71, 73, 75, 78, 79, 80, 83, 90, 91, 93, 95, 96, 97, 100.
12. स्रग्धरा 23, 25, 36, 52, 88, 99